An Awkward
Chinese
Guide to
Living Your
Best Life

An Inward Journey: A Guide To Living Your Best Life

Kelly Canull

Strategic Book Publishing
New York, New York

Copyright © 2009

All rights reserved – Kelly Canull

No part of this book may be reproduced or transmitted in any form or by any means, graphic, electronic, or mechanical, including photocopying, recording, taping, or by any information storage retrieval system, without the permission, in writing, from the publisher.

Strategic Book Publishing
An imprint of Writers Literary & Publishing Services, Inc.
845 Third Avenue, 6th Floor – 6016
New York, NY 10022

http://www.strategicbookpublishing.com

ISBN: 978-1-60860-019-9
SKU: 1-60860-019-X

Printed in the United States of America

Dedication

*I am dedicating this book to you.
Thank you for being you.*

Contents

Preface   **vii**
   The Story of the Sun vii
   How to Use This Book viii

Part One: The Big Picture   **1**
   Chapter 1: Old Paradigm vs. New Paradigm 3
   Chapter 2: Creating a Solid Foundation for
            Self-Growth 13
   Chapter 3: Awakening to the Voice of Your
            Soul on and off the Paper 25

Part Two: Moving Out of the Old Paradigm   **39**
   Chapter 4: Surrendering Who You Think
            You Are 41
   Chapter 5: Embracing Who You Really Are. 77
   Chapter 6: Responsibility/Self-Care. 95

Part Three: Living in the New Paradigm   **109**
   Chapter 7: Universal Wisdom 111
   Chapter 8: My Personal Message to You 139

Acknowledgment 155

About the Author 157

Preface

The Story of the Sun

Every morning, the sun rises in the east, and every evening, the sun sets in the west. From our point of view, it looks as though the sun is crossing over the sky from east to west. Science shows us that what is actually happening is planet Earth is revolving around the Sun. The Sun is still, while Earth revolves around it. However, what we see appears to be the sun traveling across the sky from east to west.

Life is full of stories like the sun, stories where a person may view life from a certain perspective, convinced that what she or he sees is real. Today, I am going to shift your perspective one more time. There is a universal Truth that states that there is no reality, just our perception of it. This is great news. It indicates that we have the freedom to choose which perspective we want to adopt.

As children, we viewed the world with open, imaginative, and curious eyes. Today, as adults, many of us walk around with blinders on, only seeing the world from a limited point of view. The point of this book is to show you a new way to look at your life, so that living your best life will be easy and fun and just like being a child again. Just as the Earth is actually revolving around the Sun, you are actually much more than you think you are. Join me, to move away from who you think you are, into the magnificence of Who You Really Are.

How to Use This Book

There are many different roads that will lead you inward to the Truth of Who You Really Are. This book is just one of them. This book is an invitation to your soul to awaken. It is an invitation to your mind to become still again, returning to its original form. This book has many gems of wisdom encoded within each page that will soothe the chaos of your mind and penetrate your soul to allow it to come alive once again.

This book is designed to coach you through the process of getting back in touch with your soul, so you will be empowered to live your best life. Through this process you will listen, feel, trust, and apply your soul's guidance once again. In this way, you will learn to take your power back and live from your Highest Good once again. This book does not teach dogma, spiritual practices, or belief systems.

This book is written from the purest source of Divine Love, giving you permission to stop all that you are searching for and go within. This book is an invitation inward to the seat of your soul where there is only stillness. This book will give you the tools necessary to apply the wisdom of your soul in your daily life. In this book, when I speak of your soul, feel free to replace it with any other word that you are more comfortable using, such as: God, Authentic Self, Spirit, Higher Self, Source of Your Inner Strength, Who You Really Are, Divine Essence, and the list goes on. Please just know that "soul" refers to the part of you that is greater than just your everyday personality.

There is no right or wrong way to awaken. There are no protocols, no rules, no regulations you need to follow. All it takes to awaken is your willingness to go deeper within than you are in this exact moment. Just drop inward and you will find yourself in a place you never really left. You will find what is pure, clear, innocent, and untouched by any of your life's experiences.

This book has been created as a sacred space where you can just be true to Who You Really Are. This book invites you to go to what is truly authentic for you. What is ultimately Truth, no matter where you are coming from, is what is here in every moment. This is not about any teachings that need to be learned or practices that need to be applied before you can "get" somewhere or attain some level. The Truth is that innately within you, your soul has encoded upon it exactly what serves your Highest Good to do or be in any given moment. All you are ever asked to do is surrender to this innate knowingness. When you surrender, your soul naturally rises up and guides you every step of the way. When you hold on and only listen to your mind's thoughts, you stifle the wisdom of your soul. To awaken back to your natural state is a process. This book guides you through that process, inward into the seat of your soul.

If this work is completely new to you, first take a couple of weeks to read through the book *without* doing the exercises. This will give you an overview of all the work you will be doing in the following weeks. You will be able to see the big picture first, before you break it into smaller pieces.

Each week, as you read, you will notice your entire life begin to shift. As you go through each week and do the exercises, enjoy the process of revealing to yourself Who You Really Are.

In this book, there will be certain sections that may not pertain to you because you have already done the work. If you reach a section that you have already addressed and moved through in your own life, just move on to another section.

Be patient with yourself as you read through each section. If it seems overwhelming, slow down and let everything integrate at the pace that best suits you. If you already know the lesson, teach others how to live it. It is my hope that there is a kernel of wisdom in this book for everyone. Pass through that which you are already living and spend more time in the areas that you are drawn toward. May this information be as wonderful of a journey inward for you as it has been for me.

Part One

The Big Picture

Chapter One

Old Paradigm vs. New Paradigm

Realize ...
that you have legions of angels surrounding you,
awaiting your freewill choice to invite
them into your conscious awareness.

Reintegrate ...
your inner world with your outer world.

Rejoice ...
in your magnificence.

Relieve ...
yourself from any disempowering thoughts.

Reunite ...
your Divine Mind with your human mind
and your Divine Heart with your human heart.

Do any of the following statements sound FAMILIAR to you?
- You feel deep inside that you should be doing something more, something else, but you do not know how to get started.
- You feel like your life is just not going your way.
- You are feeling depressed, anxious, guilty, or scattered in your life.
- You have glimpses of peace and tranquility, but they come and go.
- You are easily angered, stressed-out, or resentful of others.
- You are always "doing" and have no personal "you" time.
- You are constantly coming up with excuses why you cannot do something new.
- You have "let yourself go" in more than one area of your life.
- You feel guilty asking for what you really want.

If you answered "Yes" to any of the above, ask yourself if you are READY to:
- Be empowered to manifest your visions and dreams in physical ways?
- Let go of all the unhealthy relationships in your life with grace and ease?
- Understand and heal a physical ailment you may have?
- Put yourself first in an unselfish way?
- Have healthy relationships with your loved ones?
- Go back to school, start a new job, or move to a new town?
- Move forward after the loss of a loved one?
- Speak your truth and become empowered again?

If you answered "Yes" to any of the above, ask yourself if you are READY to:
- Crave simplicity in all things and require and thrive on simple processes, simple desires, and a very simple lifestyle?
- Perceive the world of different possibilities and believe all things are possible?
- Penetrate all sides of an issue, spinning ideas around to see them in a new way?
- Be agile, flexible, alert, and always ready to create?
- Feel whole, grounded, complete, and fulfilled?
- Show your true colors and have the courage to be yourself?

If you read through these lists and answered "YES, YES, YES," then this book is right for you! The reason is because you are ready to shift out of the old paradigm, and into the new.

The word paradigm describes the way we see the world in terms of our perception. On earth right now, there are two different paradigms being played out: the old paradigm and the new paradigm. You may have heard that no two people ever view the world the same way. This is because we each have our own filters that create the way we perceive the world. The object of the game of life is to continually expand the way that we view the world, moving our perceptions out of our comfort zone and into new realms of possibilities. When we do this, we move out of the old paradigm and into the new paradigm.

The old paradigm is modeled around the human mind and the lower self, coupled with fears and negativity. In fact, fear is the foundation of the old paradigm. The new paradigm, on the other hand, exists in a place where everyone lives from their Whole Self and follows the guidance of their soul, which rests on a foundation of pure Divine Love. In order to live in the new paradigm, we must cross what I call the Bridge of Remembrance, dropping all of the concepts and constraints of the old paradigm. When we cross over fully into the new paradigm, we shift the entire consciousness of this planet.

The old paradigm is where most of us currently reside. We are living our lives on autopilot, only listening to the dictates of our mental mind. As children, we believed to be real whatever was projected upon our minds by our culture, family, friends, and society. The mind's role is to keep our physical being alive. It creates stories to convince us to do certain things just to stay alive. After many years of this continuous talk, we are fully awake only to the thoughts of our mind, having covered up our Infinite Intelligence and Authentic Self, the places in us that really know where our best interests lie. The journey of this lifetime is to drop the old paradigm fully. This means we must drop all of the thoughts and projections falsely created by the mind to return home to our soul.

The new paradigm is here, and it awaits our arrival. In the new paradigm, we get to live from our deepest core. This means that all of the experiences created while we were living in the old paradigm get to fall away completely. In order to live fully in the new, we must begin listening to our Infinite Intelligence, instead of our mental thoughts, and our Divine Soul, instead of the rise and fall of our human emotions.

The new paradigm awakens within us the ultimate Truth, which is different from what we were programmed to believe. In Truth, we are already pure, radiant Beings who have within us the magnificence of Who We Really Are. So, all that we need to do to move out of the old paradigm and into the new is to drop our stories about who our mind has convinced us that we are. Then, we get to naturally awaken by allowing our True Divine Essence to arise from within us. Living in the new paradigm is about following the guidance of our soul in every moment. When we follow our own guidance, we are taking the power back that we give away every time we look outside of ourselves for guidance.

What do you say I show you a few examples of how you will experience your life when you are living in the new paradigm and following your own innate wisdom? In the new paradigm:

- You remain focused on your own personal mission for being on earth.
- You remain focused on the positive path of your life.
- You are a part of a bigger community of people who are creating an ideal spiritual culture and living Heaven here on earth.
- You have no enemies. You see that others are souls of Light who are just playing out their part perfectly so you may know Thy Divine Self better.
- You begin to feel the beauty of Who You Really Are, which inspires you to awaken more fully to your individual purpose and gifts.
- As you live a life of a walking meditation, you become an open valve through which your guidance will flow daily.
- You stop looking to others outside of yourself for guidance and began to really trust your own innate wisdom.
- You no longer settle for less than what you feel innately is your calling.
- Naturally, you move towards the job that supports the expression of Who You Are.
- You begin to call in support and love into your life. You are ready to live from a place of unity amongst community.
- You are 100 percent in your integrity. You are open and honest with all of your relationships. When you are

living from a place of integrity, you draw like-minded people into your inner circle.
- You attract a new mate, or you and your current partner create a spiritual partnership where there are no more old wounds to heal. Instead, you love, admire, and adore one another without any dependencies.
- There is a complete absence of fear because you feel a deep sense of peace and calm.

Imagine a new paradigm where you are free to express your Divine Essence by living fully integrated as your Whole Self. Through the greatest imaginings come the inspiration, motivation, and empowerment to fully live on earth with our fullest potential. Let us begin to explore what this new world will look and feel like. Come, lay your mind at the door of your heart and let the music of your soul sing a tune that comes from your inner core. The vibration is so pure, serene, and quaint that it calls upon your body to rest and allow the door of infinite wisdom to open.

Travel with me on this journey inward to the roadmap of your soul. It is time for the pure love that is inside of you to come out and play. Together, let's shift the paradigm out of the old model based on fear and embrace the new one founded in Divine Love. Imagine with me as we dance through insights into a new wave of our Being. It is a new wave because we are imagining that the current model of your life is not serving your Highest Good any longer. This new model of Self is where you are free to imagine beyond the constraints of the human mind and live out your greatest dreams. The way to live your life fully in the new paradigm is to discard the foundation of the old paradigm. This new world model is where you are supported and honored for living the experience of your soul and living fully empowered as your Highest Good.

The Big Picture

Let's imagine that you are driving to a specific destination and you find that you are LOST. There is no one around from whom you might ask for directions, and you left your roadmap, cell phone, and GPS system at home. Now, what happens? Do you keep driving around, hoping that you will find what you are looking for, or would you be willing to try something new?

What would you say if I told you that you had the resources within you to ask yourself a question every day and receive clarity and guidance in regard to that question within 24 hours of asking? Would you ask the question? Would you be open to receiving the clarity and guidance in response to your question? I know just how crippling feeling lost, confused, and uncertain of which way to go can be. I know how frustrating it is to pray and feel like you are not heard. I know how living from your fears can destroy your family, your career, your life. I know how feeling lost and confused, unsure of your future and fearful of the unknown, can put a strangle hold on your life—-squeezing your hopes and dreams right out of you.

The good news is that innately within you is your own personal roadmap, compliments of your soul. The roadmap of your soul will always show you where to go and how to get there with 100% accuracy. You see, your soul knows exactly what purpose you have for being on this planet. Your soul can give you the directions on how to live from your Highest Self, in any given moment. Your soul can show you how to let go of all that no longer benefits you, so that you can live in alignment with your true passions.

There is one universal Truth that unites all of us on this planet: We are all here to **LIVE** out our own unique purpose for being on earth. Right now, millions of us are walking around with the wisdom of our souls buried inside of us; this wisdom is an untapped resource waiting to be discovered.

This life that you are living offers a free choice between Divine Love and fear. It is a choice between listening to the dictates of your mind or following the powerful guidance of your soul. Your soul, as Divine Love, is present no matter what rises and falls in your daily life. Your mind, on the other hand, is where fear sleeps. Your soul is where Divine Love exists. In every moment, you are offered an opportunity to choose Divine Love over fear. You are offered an opportunity to listen, feel, and apply the guidance of your soul, or simply ignore it. This is your free will: the freedom to choose between following the guidance of your soul or the dictates of your mind.

Here is the BIG UNIVERSAL PICTURE:
- Each of us has a soul.
- Each of us has a unique purpose for being on earth, which is encoded upon our soul.
- Every day, we have an opportunity to ask our soul for clarity, guidance, and direction.
- Our soul will always show us an answer to our prayers, requests, questions, or inquiries.

A New Perspective:
Our souls have important messages for us to receive, but in order to do this, we must be willing to stop and ask for direction. By stopping and asking, we will innately remember how to listen, feel, and live out the guidance of our soul. Our soul is our own personal guide. It is the one Source that will always be there for us. It is the one Light that will always shine in support of us following and fulfilling our dreams. Its job is to show us how to live from our Authentic Self. Our intuition is the gateway to the One Source from which we all originated.

Throughout our entire lifetime, our intuition has always been within us, awaiting our arrival. We have had glimpses of our intuition guiding us, but once we actually claim it as our own, we open up the gateway to receiving the clarity and guidance that will help us in every aspect of our lives.

If we are going to co-create a new paradigm founded in love, then it is essential to create an internal bond with our intuition. If we are not establishing Divine Love, our highest essence, within ourselves first, then we should not expect to see it play out in our outer reality.

This life is about being empowered. Remember that our external reality is highly affected by our internal vibrations, meaning that what we experience on the outside is what we feel inside. So much of our energy is wasted on trying to change our external circumstances. An empowered being chooses to create from the inside, out. An empowered being creates an internal bond with the Divine Essence of Who They Really Are. We have to start living in a new way, a way where we trust our inner guidance and stop going outside of ourselves for clarity. Creating an internal bond is about returning to a space of trust. When we do not trust our heart, we all too often maintain our defense mechanisms and old patterns of being wounded. This causes us to remain in a false prison of our minds. With trust, we can once again feel a deep connection to the Source of our inner strength and ask for the energies of Divine Love to fill us up. Our soul, our Divine Guidance, is within us, and only we can access it. When we start to listen inward to our heart and soul, we will be living fully in the new paradigm founded in Divine Love. This freedom will be felt within us as we choose to free ourselves from the bonds of the mind, and instead, bond with the essence of our Divinity. When we start to commune again with our innate wisdom, that wisdom is going to be elated and show us exactly where and how we can follow its guidance.

Our inner guidance has so much to show us that our minds will never understand. Our inner guidance has a love for us so grand that there are no words to describe it; it is a love that goes beyond any words.

This is a path for the Spiritual Warrior. It takes courage and strength to walk this path of the unknown. It also takes more energy to stay in our negative mindsets than it does to simply let them go. Your thoughts are tricky, as they work intently on maneuvering away from your intuition, the source of your Divine Essence, so you will not trust it. The first thing you need to do to learn to follow your intuition is to be willing to stop the thoughts of your mind and open up to the flow of your intuition. If you are willing to be still just for one moment, you will feel that what you have feared is actually just Divine Love. When you become still, you will recognize the Truth of your Being. To trust your intuition, you must begin inviting it into your consciousness.

This is the time for you to fully embrace your spiritual body. It will feel unfamiliar at first, as all new things do. Yet, now is the time to take a risk and bow out of the old paradigm where fear-based thoughts ruled our world. The world needs our full presence on this earth as fully integrated souls.

Are you ready to live a more dynamic and fulfilling life where you are able to clearly receive the messages that your soul is sending you? Are you ready to follow the roadmap of your soul, instead of feeling lost and confused? If so, then let's continue to move forward on this inward journey. Your soul deserves this chance to come out and shine its brilliant light once again.

Chapter Two

Creating a Solid Foundation for Self-Growth

Remake ...
your old wounds into new creations that empower you.

Regain ...
your courage to live your life to its fullest.

Reclaim ...
your birthright of abundance that will come in all forms.

Redirect ...
your life so that you are living from a place of integrity.

Stilling the Mind

We are at a critical time in history where the old foundation of fear is crumbling and we need to collectively create a new foundation of living as our Whole Self, founded in Divine Love. In order to do this, we must invite our dialoging mind into silence. We cannot hear our soul when we are too busy talking to ourselves. Our fears are a creation only of the mind. By stilling the mind, we invite it back inward into absolute silence, the place from which it was born. Through the process of stillness, the mind gets to fall back into love with its natural essence: the soul. Each practice that I lay before you is intended to do just that. Each practice is intended to invite your fears inward into your soul.

The following is a daily routine with seven exercises created as a means to living as your Whole Self. This foundation builds a solid place on which you may rest as you continue to move inward to the Truth of Who You Really Are. Without a solid foundation, you will most likely return to doing things the same way that you have always done them and you won't receive the results that your heart desires. So, I invite you to follow this morning practice for at least sixty days. Eventually, you can simply use only what you love, incorporating your own natural rituals into the practice.

To Get Started: Create an Altar

This morning routine is about stilling your mind, sending out your prayers (a form of asking your soul) to the universe, and being open to receive your guidance. This morning routine is intended to be used in conjunction with everything I teach you about rediscovering the roadmap of your soul. A beautiful starting point to living your life from a place of peace and serenity is to create an altar. An altar is a sacred space where you can sit and go inward for peace and tranquility. There are no rules as to how this altar has to be made, except that it is a comfortable, quiet, clean space where you can sit for at least fifteen minutes. Create it in a corner of your bedroom, a space in your kitchen, or anywhere that you know will be a quiet space to sit. If you are traveling, you can even create a traveling altar to bring with you.

On your altar, you can start out with pictures of loved ones, a candle, a favorite poem or symbol, or anything else that makes you feel good. There are also books about creating altars that can give you more ideas. Be creative. Inquire within: What does unconditional love look like? Create your altar to look like unconditional love. Keep the space free from any clutter on, or surrounding, it. I invite you to create this sacred space around your altar to represent the new you.

Next, Reawaken Your Divine Essence

Now that you have created an altar where you can practice discipline, I will show you where to go from here on your path of self-love. Remember that what I share with you is just one of many ways to design your daily routine. Yet, I advise you to start with this practice as a roadmap. You can easily make adjustments as you go along.

Every day, when you wake up, I would like for you to sit down in front of your altar. Initially, when you wake up, your mind will go on autopilot and try to convince you that you do not have the time to do any silly morning routine since you have a huge "to do" list waiting for you to accomplish. All too often, we get stuck on autopilot mode. We wake up and go, fulfilling our "to do" list, without putting much conscious thought into our day. Let me remind you that you have been living on autopilot for a very long time. As you practice your new routine each day, the light of awareness will gradually be turned on. Once it has been turned on, it is impossible to turn off. This is good news because when your inner light is illuminated, it makes remembering Who You Really Are so much easier. However, if you expend all of your time and energy trying to turn your awareness off, you soon find yourself worn out. When you inquire within, you will naturally feel an inner resistance. The only way to face this resistance is to deal with it head on. Only when you remain present, through whatever arises, will you really be able to feel the benefits. When this happens, I suggest before going any further, you take a moment to assess the situation. Your mind wants to have control and make you so busy that you will have too many excuses to practice, whereas your soul is simply asking for your presence for just 15 minutes every morning. Remember, in order for you to live from your Divine Essence, you will have to try something new.

The next eight steps are to be done every morning in chronological order. I have given you a brief explanation, followed by what you will want to say at each point, in italics. The entire morning routine should only take fifteen minutes.

1. Set Your Intention for the Day

An intention is something that you are consciously choosing to focus your attention on. Setting an intention draws your conscious mind into the forefront. It is a declaration of what you consciously want to create in your day. It allows you to focus your attention on what you do want, instead of walking around on autopilot experiencing, all too often, what you do not want.

When we go outside each day, we see the sun shining billions of rays of light all over the earth. As a child, do you remember taking a magnifying glass and using the sun's rays to burn a hole in a piece of paper? This is an example of focus. All too often, however, we live without focus, direction, or purpose. We wake up each day with our thoughts all over the place.

Setting an intention causes the universal energy to focus, creating an energetic path that supports your intention, like a stream creating different tributaries. By stating an intention, you ensure that the river knows which path to flow down miles before you reach the intersection. Our intentions set the stage for the life we are leading. Setting our intention on a daily basis means that we have decided to be more conscious and aware of what our life looks like and where we are going on our journey of self-discovery. Intent is a powerful force for creation and manifestation. It is the application of the power of Divine Will toward creating a specific outcome.

The following is a list of intentions that may help you think about the intentions you would like to set for the day:

It is my intention to:
    Eat healthier (tangible)
    Live my Highest Good (intangible)
    Buy a new car that is a hybrid to save the earth's ozone layer (tangible)
    Be more positive today (intangible)
    Look at life from a new perspective (intangible)
    Laugh more with my children (tangible)

What I would like for you to do is to write out three intangible intentions and three tangible intentions. Place these cards on your bathroom mirror, on your steering wheel, on your desk at work, or anywhere you can see them throughout your day. These are your intentions for the day. Recite them out loud, or in your head, throughout the day.

2. Focus Your Thoughts through Candle Gazing

By practicing this candle gazing exercise daily, you will produce focus once again in your life.

You will need to get a candle (preferably soy-based) and a timer.

Place your candle on your altar, a few feet in front of you. For the first two weeks, set your timer for five minutes. After two weeks, increase the time to ten minutes. Start to stare/gaze into the candle.

As you do this, be conscious of your thoughts. Your mind will begin its normal chatter, filled with what you should be, could be, need to be doing, doing, doing. Allow these thoughts to come up, and then set them free. Be with this exercise and do not engage in any of the thoughts that arise. Allow your mind to be cleared, and empty of thought. Focus on the candle. Treat it like you are driving a car: When your attention gets pulled away from the candle, redirect it back to the flame. As your thoughts come up, imagine they are just clouds in the sky passing by. Do not dialogue with them, just let them pass by. Put your focus on the gap, as if there is white space in between these black words, and place your attention on the intervals in between your thoughts. This is Who You Really Are.

Candle gazing is a wonderful way to become more aware of your thoughts. Notice how scattered your thoughts are. Did you find that you wanted to fall asleep? Did the flame move up and down according to where your thoughts were going? Was five minutes a long time?

As you continue to use this tool day after day, you will begin to notice how your thoughts start to still themselves. The point of this exercise is to help you gain control of your thoughts again. It is a way for you to see that after first stilling your thoughts, you can then decide which ones you want to keep and which ones you wish to discard.

Later on, I will show you how your thoughts are creating your reality, but first, quieting your mind is essential if you want to listen to the messages of your soul, and doing this morning routine is the way to get there.

3. Alignment Prayer

Prayers hold a vibration of pure love. By sending out our prayers daily, we are sending out our requests to the universe and are becoming conscious co-creators of our world. Our prayers are heard and felt all across the universe. Creating a regular prayer routine is a great way to move out of autopilot mode, and into self-awareness.

The following is an example of a prayer that you may send out during your daily routine. It is entitled: The Alignment Prayer. The intention of the prayer is to align your lower self with your Higher Self, as God's Will and your will are one. Every prayer represents a request that you are sending forth through your heart into the hands of the Divine Source of your inner strength. Feel free to substitute in your own prayer, or you may enjoy using this one:

Recite the following out loud or to yourself:
> *I release all that no longer serves my Highest Good and I open up to all that serves my Highest Good and the Highest Good of All That Is.*
> *I pray for guidance, clarity, wisdom, and understanding.*
> *I am a pure radiant light. I am fulfilling thy divine purpose Now.*
> *Teach me what I need to learn,*
> *Show me what I need to see,*
> *Take me where I need to go,*
> *Tell me what I need to hear.*
> *Give me the compassion, conviction, and the courage to do All that is in my Highest Good.*
> *I ask for this or something better, for the Highest Good Of All That Is.*
> *Thy Will Be Done and So It Is.*

4. "I AM" Affirmations

Creating clear "I AM" affirmations affirms your intention about where you want your thoughts to go. As the arrow once said to its archer, "Wherever you aim me, I will go," stating affirmations directs your arrow to the target of thoughts that are the most productive for you. This is very similar to stating your intention. You could state your intention to be a more loving person today and your "I AM" affirmation could support it by saying "I am a loving person."

Here are a few more examples:
  I am in alignment with my Highest Good.
  I trust the unfolding of my Divine purpose.
  I am a more loving parent.
  I am already whole, pure, and beautiful.
  I am letting go of my judgments.
  I am successful.
  I am spending more alone time to take care of me.
  I am standing in my integrity.

Create three of your own "I AM" affirmations for today and write them out. Place these where you can see them throughout your day. Recite them to yourself every time you see them.

5. Gratitude

Gratitude, plus anything, always equals love. Gratitude is a flow of universal abundance, a giving and receiving process of All That Is and All That May Be. When we express gratitude, we are giving love back to the Universe, establishing a flow of energy between our Self and the source of all things. Gratitude is the recognition of the flow between us and the universe. Show your gratitude to life through the celebration of love, severance, and bliss. Be grateful for your lessons, your life, and your creations. Be grateful for every experience that has brought you to this point in your life. Be grateful for the opportunity to learn more. Be grateful for all that you have received and all that is to come. Remain in a state of gratitude for all that you have, have had, and desire to create.

Gratitude + Anger = Love
Gratitude + Guilt = Love
Gratitude + Fear = Love

When we are fully integrated into a state of gratitude, we are home. Home is where the truth of Who We Really Are resides. Gratitude awakens our dormant energies and floods us with high vibrations of Divine Love.

Gratitude actually affects our brain chemistry and health. It can be utilized in connecting deeper into sacred relationships with our Self and others. Gratitude is a high vibration that attunes to the vibrations of peace, Divine Love, joy, and bliss. When you state your gratitude list, get in touch with how it makes you feel. It will dissolve all lower vibrations, negative emotions, and old patterns.

I have placed a space for your gratitude list in your morning routine for a reason. If you state out loud one thing you are grateful for every day, watch how the law of attraction (discussed in the next chapter) will continue to bring you just that.

Here are a few examples:
   I am grateful for my health.
   I am grateful for all that I do have.
   I am grateful for my family.
   I am grateful for this opportunity to rediscover the roadmap of my soul.

Now create your own list. Today, I am grateful for (fill in the blank) ...

6. Call in the Source of Your Inner Strength
At this stage, it is time to invite in the Source of your inner strength that surrounds you every day. You are the master of

your own domain. So, feel free to call in God, the masters, saints, your Higher Self, your angels, your spirit guides, your soul, or whatever represents pure love to you. What really matters is that you are connecting in with the Source of your inner strength. Whatever name you choose is fine. Source awaits your invitation to come more fully into your life. All you need is a pure intention to ask the Source of your inner strength to come into your life today and guide you each day forward. This practice allows you to call upon your soul to guide you.

You do not need to wait until a time when you are desperate to call in the Divine. You can ask to connect with the roadmap of your soul at any time. This morning routine is designed for you to invite the Divine Source into your life each and every day. You have learned about how your soul communicates with you. Now you are just calling forth your soul, letting it know that you await its guidance.

Now call in the Source of your Inner Strength. Here is an example of what you can say:

Divine Source of my Inner Strength, please surround me with your love. I ask my soul to continue guiding me. Give me a sign today that shows me whether I am on the right path, or not. Either way, I call forth this Divine Love to fill my heart today.

7. Communicating with the Voice of Your Soul

Communicating with the Voice of Your Soul involves having a never-ending, direct conversation with the Voice of Your Soul each day. I will spend the entire next chapter showing you how you can use writing as a way to drop into your Theta brain wave pattern and access the Voice of Your Soul directly, but before we move on to that important and final step in this daily routine, I would like to reinforce the idea of routine and practice.

Integrating a daily spiritual practice into your life is a breath of fresh air for your soul. You will want to start off by doing this daily routine every morning before ending your day with communicating with the Voice of Your Soul. Do this for thirty consecutive days. Research shows that once we choose a new habit and stick with it for thirty consecutive days, we create new neural pathways in our brain; this is how we let go of old, non-productive habits and consciously create new, empowering ones. When you commit to this daily routine, you awaken all aspects of your Highest Self that may be lying dormant within. It is up to you to start living your life from a new perspective. This model shows you how to easily focus your attention inward. After just one day of focusing within, you will begin to see how your outer reality starts to slow down to become more peaceful once again.

Life is always going to happen. Creating a daily routine helps you to manage your life because you are able to live from a new, more open, and peaceful perspective. With this new perspective, you will see your mind naturally becomes more still and allows space for your Divine Essence to be felt and heard. Remember that it is essential to still the mind in order to hear your soul.

Let me recap the seven steps to your routine. Feel free to write this list out for yourself and place it on your altar.

1. Set your Intention

2. Candle Gazing

3. Alignment Prayer

4. "I AM" Affirmation

5. Gratitude

6. Call in the Source of Your Inner Strength

7. Communicating with the Voice of Your Soul

Follow me, now, as I show you how you can awaken the Voice of Your Soul and start asking it all of your heartfelt questions, so that you can receive the clarity and guidance in your life today that will help you gain a greater understanding of Who You Really Are.

Chapter Three

Awakening to the Voice of Your Soul On, and Off, the Paper

There are many ways that your soul chooses to communicate with you. You see, your soul will have a unique way of showing you what you are to do, or not do, in any given moment. Your soul communicates with you by using the diversity of the universe. Your soul resides in a world where it can see much more than what your limited conscious mind can see. The objective is for you to have daily, direct, and never-ending conversations with your soul so that you can know what it knows, see what it sees, and live your life from a more aware point of view.

Your soul is ready and waiting for you to initiate a conversation with it, so it can share with you the wisdom of a new, greater perspective than your mind could ever imagine. Your soul is ready, and I am here to share with you how you can talk to your soul so that it will compassionately listen to you. As it listens, it sends wisdom and guidance back your way. Normally, life is like shooting an arrow with our wishes, wants, and prayers up to the sky. We hope that something is listening, and someday will answer our prayers. In the meantime, we turn to friends or our journals or a family member to confide in, while, inwardly, we may feel frantic and stressed-out. We do not know which road to choose, and we cannot fully reveal everything to someone else for fear they may judge us. You see, when you share your full story—feelings and all—with your soul, it listens to you with a deep, compassionate ear. It does not judge, distort, nor interrupt you while you dig in deep and reveal your deepest secrets, wishes, and wants. Your soul looks forward to these conversations each day because it knows that deep inside, you are ready to let go of these feelings and thoughts so you can make room for more enriching ideas and emotions.

In this model of awakening to the Voice of Your Soul, you will be using a specific writing technique that will activate the Voice of Your Soul for you. You will find yourself expressing aspects of your thoughts that may have been with you since birth. This technique gives you a space to free pent up emotions that might even have been causing illness because they were not allowed to flow freely. The best mantra is to free-flow your feelings to freedom. This technique allows this to happen effortlessly and joyfully.

Getting back in touch with your soul is just like having a running conversation with a great friend. The point of this book is to show you that you can begin turning inward to your soul for clarity and guidance in your life. It is my intention that this process be liberating. It is your birthright to ask for, and receive, clarity upon any subject, question, concern, thought, etc. going on in your life.

If you recall, this technique is used in your sacred morning routine. You will be seated at your altar. You will have stated your intention, stared at the candle, affirmed your "I AM" and gratitude statements, aligned with a prayer, and called on the Source of your Inner Strength, all in preparation for this next part where you will be communicating with the Voice of Your Soul.

Here is what you will need at your altar for this next part:
   a. Pen
   b. Notebook (Paper)
   c. Glass of water
   d. Something to stimulate your Sense of Smell (candle, incense, flowers)
   e. Quiet Sacred Space
   f. Privacy

MORNING ROUTINE + ACTIVATING ALL 5 SENSES + WRITING FAST = ACTIVATING THE VOICE OF YOUR SOUL

A) Morning Routine—Follow the morning routine mentioned in the previous chapter. By committing to the same time and place (your altar) to perform your morning routine, you will make listening to your soul easier.

Below, I will share with you what you will be doing at Step 7 of your morning routine, called: Communicating with the Voice of Your Soul. (Remember you have already gone through Steps 1–6). *Now:*

1. *Breathe deeply a few times.*

2. *Take a sip of your water.*

3. *Set your verbal intention to communicate with the Voice of Your Soul.*

   Ex: Dear Soul, I am here ready to connect with your Voice. I am ready, willing, and excited to hear what you have to share. I thank you in advance for your love and wisdom today.
   or
   Dearest Soul—
   I am ready to reconnect with you. It is my intention to align my body, mind, and soul so that the wisdom of my soul has

a clear path in which to send its messages. I am going to be clearing my mind of all of the distractions that keep me from receiving your guidance. Please give me the courage to move forward. Please continue to send your messages to me, even if I do not receive them easily to begin with. I am fully committed to listening, feeling, trusting, and applying the wisdom that you have to share with me. I am open to seeing or feeling the presence of my soul once again. Blessed Be.

B) Activating all 5 Senses—Dropping into theta waves:

Next, you will want to make sure your sense of smell is stimulated with a scented candle, incense, essential oils, fresh flowers, or something else that resonates with you. As you sit ready to write to your soul with your sense of smell activated, take a drink of water. These steps activate all five senses at the same time and drop you into a theta-wave pattern where you are able to access your soul.

Pen to paper—Activates Auditory, Visual, and Kinesthetic Senses

Scented candle, incense, flowers, etc.—Activates Olfactory Senses

Water—Activates Taste Sense

C) Writing Very Fast—Writing down your story and asking lots of questions:

You are seated in your sacred space, have set your intention, had a sip of water, and now you start your letter. The key to your letter is that as you start writing, all of your writing is to be done very fast—-so fast that you may not even be able to read your own handwriting. This is ok.

If you would like to take a moment and reflect inward on a few questions, here are some good examples:

What is happening to me right now? What is on my mind right now? What is bothering me right now? What is keeping me up at night? What am I worrying about? Where do my thoughts repeatedly go when I am alone? What am I afraid of? What have I been praying for the most about recently? What old pains are still tying my stomach in knots? What am I frustrated about? What am I sad about? What do I really want to share that I have not disclosed to anyone before? What challenges am I facing right now?

Start by taking the pen and paper, and write out a salutation:

Dear Soul (you can change this to whatever name resonates with you),

Below this, you will start to write about whatever—YES, WHATEVER!—you feel like writing about. This is where you bring anything and everything to the paper, literally. It is best to **write both your thoughts and your feelings** around what is going on for you.

Start with what is going on for you right now, today. Start with where you are. Write what comes. Explore your deepest thoughts and feelings. Tell the Truth. Write really fast. Ignore all writing rules (no editing). Speak from your heart. It is through writing that you will open your spiritual ear. Let the writing go where the writing wants to go. Your story is your healer so TELL THE UNEDITED VERSION OF YOUR STORY!

Now, after you have shared, vented, purged, and released all that you want to say, the next part is where you ask your soul a question. The key is to ask lots of questions. When you ask your soul a question, keep writing as soon as you ask the question; this is where your soul comes alive and talks back to you. Remember, all of your writing is done very fast. It is not your mind talking; instead, it is the Voice of Your Soul. The intention alone has activated the Voice of Your Soul. By activating all five senses, you drop into a theta brain wave where you get to see your world from the perspective of your soul.

After you ask a question and get a response, you can keep asking questions and go deeper with your conversation. When you feel complete, you can say thank you to your soul, and end your letter.

Below I have given you a first person description of how this practice will look:

I am choosing to sit for a minimum of 15 minutes every day for a minimum of 30 consecutive days. I sit at my beautiful altar with my pen, paper, glass of water, and sense of smell being stimulated by my _____ (incense, essential oils, flowers, scented candle, etc).

I thank my soul verbally and let it know that I intend for us to have a fabulous conversation together today.

*I take a sip of my water, breathe in and out deeply a few times, and start to write very **fast**——*

I communicate with my soul, and it listens:

"Dear Soul,

(My story for the day goes here) *I write down both my feelings and my thoughts*

(My question goes here)

(Guidance/Insights/Wisdom from my soul goes here—my soul is communicating with me and I am listening) *I write any insights legibly in columns or in another notebook*

I listen with my spiritual/mystical ear.

(Next question goes here)

(Guidance/Insights/Wisdom from my soul goes here—I trust this is my soul and not my mind talking to me) *I write any insights legibly in columns or in another notebook*

I listen with my spiritual/mystical ear.

I feel complete and offer Gratitude to my soul and take a sip of my water."

I wrote very fast without editing, judging, fixing or stopping. Some pretty interesting stuff came up. I will sit with it all for today.

This example shows you how you can have direct, never-ending conversations with the Voice of Your Soul, on paper everyday.

Next, I will give you some examples of questions or statements you can ask your soul:

- *What job better suits me?*
- *How do I move through this divorce with understanding, compassion, and ease?*
- *What is in my best interest to do for my child in this situation?*
- *How do I attract into my life new, healthy relationships?*
- *What do I need to do to stop smoking?*
- *How can I have a better relationship with my parents or children?*
- *What is in alignment with my Highest Good to do today?*
- *How can I attract the resources so that I can change my life's path?*
- *What do I need to let go of so that I have more "me" time?*

or

Dearest Soul,
Show me a sign today in alignment with what serves my Highest Good.

or

Higher Self,
I have a question that I would like to ask: _____.
  Please give me clarity and guidance around this subject today. I am open to receive the answer.

or

Divine Highest Good,
Please surround me today with the brilliant white light of love. I am open to allow all that serves my Highest Good to flow into my life. I release all that no longer serves my Highest Good to be transmuted and return to its original form of love. Give me the strength to keep my awareness open. I ask to be shown today what I need to see. I honor my intuition and my Highest Self to teach me what I need to learn today. Thy Will be done, and so it is.

or

I call upon my Higher Self, my soul, God, and all the pure love that surrounds me.

Please help me to integrate these new principles and guidelines for my life. I am open to letting go, yet my mind still feels pretty powerful. Please continue to send me the strength to go within and listen to the guidance of my soul. Open up my heart so that I feel purpose behind all that I am doing. Let this be a new level of awareness for me.

or

I invite my angels forth to guide me. I trust the guidance that I am receiving.

Today show me a sign that I am on the right path. If I am not on the path of my Highest Good, please show me gracefully how I can return back to the path of my Divine Essence. I am open to receive this guidance and invite more light and love into my life.

or

Divine Higher Self,
Here are my dreams, desires, goals and aspirations. I trust that they will unfold in Divine Timing in alignment with my Highest Good. If there are lessons that I need to receive right now, before my dreams will manifest, I am open to receive them. Give me the courage to move through any adversity. Give me patience to sur-

render to Divine Timing. Show me what it is that I need to see right now. I trust that what I am shown is in my Highest Good for me to face. I let go and let God. Blessed Be.

Communicating with the Voice of Your Soul develops an eternal bond between you and your soul: Your soul listens, and it communicates back to you, and you listen too. As I mentioned earlier, too often, we are in the habit of sending out an arrow to the heavens wishing and wanting, without real results. However, in the technique outlined here, you will experience your arrow like a boomerang: You will send out your thoughts, prayers, and feelings, and your soul will communicate right back to you, just like the boomerang that always returns.

Here is the new paradigm where we get to have an open line of communication between our conscious mind's limited point of view and the infinite views that our soul gets to see. In this new paradigm, we learn how to listen to the Voice of Our Soul with a compassionate ear. We get to pay more attention to how our soul is speaking to us, both on and off the paper.

One of the most amazing things about a daily commitment to communicating directly to the Voice of Your Soul on paper is that your soul's communication to you *off* the paper becomes even more detailed and obvious.

Awakening to the voice of the soul allows us the grace of receiving clarity on any subject, at any time that we decide to focus on it. When we use the paper, we are turning the phone lines of communication back on. After we are done writing for the day, and go about our daily life, our soul is still present, and in constant communication with us.

Once you start your daily practice of sitting and writing to your soul, it answers you right there on the paper. Remember that by committing to your morning routine, you are initiating a never-ending conversation where you receive guidance from your soul both on, and off, the paper. Let's move forward now, so I can share with you ways that your soul loves to communicate with you off the paper.

Your soul loves to use all the resources in your world to show you other messages. When you use the morning routine of communicating to your soul, you often will receive confirmation of your soul's insights throughout the day. Below, I have described a few examples of signs of soul communication for you. The intention is for this list is to stimulate your awareness so that you can honor the signs when they show up for you.

Messages may appear in these forms:
- Signs—a star, a feather, a penny, a phone call.
- Symbols—a heart, a ring, a diamond, a butterfly, a rainbow.
- Messages From Others—You may receive messages from what others have to say or from a passage in a book. Pay attention: Many times there is a message in it for you.
- Auditory Hearing (Voice of Your Soul)—You may hear your soul talk to you in a sweet, loving, and empowering voice that gives you directions.
- Music—Pay attention to lyrics or maybe a favorite song that comes on at just the right moment.
- Animals—Each animal represents something bigger than just its appearance. There are many books that share the message behind the totem of the animals. *Animal Speak* by Ted Andrews is one of my favorites.
- Your Body—Your body can tell you a lot about what is going on. Louise Hay has many books (ex. *You Can Heal Your Life)* that show you a deeper meaning behind

many physical conditions and what you can do to change them.
- Dreams—Dreams can be prophetic, help you solve a problem, be etheric, or they can bring you clarity and guidance in your life.
- Visions—What may appear to be daydreaming many times has a lot of guidance in it.

The whole universe is used every day by your soul to communicate its messages to you. Below, I invite you to participate actively with the Voice of Your Soul.

SYMBOLS

One of the ways that your soul sends you messages is through symbols. The following exercise allows you to consciously choose a symbol whose appearance will provide confirmation that your soul is communicating with you.

1. This exercise is about creating a personal symbol with which you can identify. Choose a symbol today that represents something to you. For example: a dime, a feather, a penny, rainbows, your favorite animal, favorite song, a color, a feeling, a loved one, or anything with which you already resonate with, and love.
2. Now, you are going to make a pact with your soul that when you see that symbol or sign, it will be a message reassuring you that you are on the right path. All you have to do is say:
   Soul,
   I am choosing (a)_____ as my sign for now. Please bring this sign or symbol into my life to reassure me that I am not alone, and that I am supported and loved. When I see the sign, I will honor it and feel how loved I really am. If my

interpretation is not correct, please continue to send me messages in a clear way so that I am clear about what you are telling me. I trust this guidance and am grateful for it daily.

Watch how often your symbol appears in your life over the next few days. As you receive signs and symbols, it will be up to you to begin understanding the message and meaning behind them. This takes practice. Honor your guidance by acknowledging when you receive a sign or symbol.

SIGNS

The following is another exercise in which you consciously use the symbols and signs all around you as another way to pay attention to how your soul is communicating with you. You will need a piece of paper and a pen.

1. On the top of your paper, I would like for you to ask a question. It can be anything. For example, you might just ask what is in your Highest Good to know. After you have written down your question, turn the paper over.

2. Next, you are going to look around the room or area where you are sitting. One object will stick out more than any other. When you have found that object, I want you to just look at it for a minute.

3. Now, place the pen on the paper as you look at the object and begin letting your thoughts go away, as you write from your heart. This method is called stream of consciousness writing. Let the object stimulate your heart, and begin writing down whatever is coming up for you. Continue writing until you feel inside that you are complete.

4. Next, turn your paper back over, and re-read your question. Then, turn the paper back over, and read the answer to the question you wrote. If the connection between your question and the symbol is not obvious to you at first, read between the lines. Give it some time, and be conscious of what the symbol's message is to you. Practice this exercise daily as you continue to see the connection between your soul and symbols.

5. I would like for you now to recite the following:
Divine Soul,
Please continue to bring me guidance with this question throughout the next few days. I am open to receiving clarity as I pay attention to different signs and symbols that are clearly sent for me. I am grateful.

Surrender, and watch how you are divinely guided over the next few days. What you just experienced was a combination of stream of conscious writing and the use of symbols. Stream of conscious writing is a way to get out of your own way and let your soul give you clarity and guidance. Next, you are going to do an exercise where you ask your soul to communicate to you through your dreams.

DREAMS
The following exercise is for you to do before you go to bed.

Place a journal next to your bedside. Every night before you go to bed, you can recite the following:

Divine Soul,
I am ready to start recalling my dreams. Please help me write out what I do remember. Give me the strength to stay with this discipline. I am very interested in connecting more fully with the Truth

of Who I Really Am. I see that recalling my dreams is one great way to do that. I invite my Highest Wisdom into my dreams so I can easily recall them.

Initially you may not recall every dream. Be patient with this process. All that matters is that you set the intention to use your dreams as a way to receive guidance from your soul. As you practice, you will begin to recall certain parts of your dreams. Remember also that messages from dreams come through symbols. Always ask your soul during the day what each symbol represents. There are also many great dream interpretation books. My favorite is: *The Mystical, Magical, Marvelous World of Dreams* by Wilda B. Tanner.

So far, I have shown you the nuts and bolts of how to listen to the Voice of Your Soul. If you would like to learn more about the technique I call, Awakening to the Voice of Your Soul, I highly recommend you read a fabulous book called: *Writing Down Your Soul: How to Activate and Listen to the Extraordinary Voice Within*, by Janet Conner. She dedicates her entire book to breaking this technique down and sharing with us the science as well as the mystic behind this amazing way that we can all awaken to the voice of our souls.

In the following chapters, I will take you back into your past where you will bring to the surface some of your old conditioning. Your mind will always want to be in control of your life unless you learn how to embrace and honor it. Remember that we are currently residing in the old paradigm and are moving forward into the new. The "meat" of your work will be in letting go of the limitations that your mind has put on you and opening up to the Infinite Light of Who You Really Are. Only your soul can show you how to live in the new paradigm as Divine Love. So, let's move inward to where your mind can be still again, inward to where your soul has a voice, where your true passion and joy lies, and where you will feel at home, once again.

Part Two

Moving Out of the Old Paradigm

Chapter Four

Surrendering Who You Think You Are

Reinvent ...
your life: Live from the seat of your soul, the heart.

Reflect ...
upon this question, "Who Am I?"

Retrieve ...
your spirit from within.

Refocus ...
your aim. "Wherever you aim me, I will go,"
says the arrow to its archer.

Awareness is about being present in the moment. Awareness is about moving out of autopilot mode and into a state of participating in your life as a co-creator. In order for you to move fully into the new paradigm, you will need to address personal wounds created in the old paradigm. You will need to see that you are not your mind. In the last chapter, you learned how to create a solid foundation where you began stilling the thoughts of your mind, a step which will help you through this next phase. Everything from this point forward is about releasing your hold on who you thought you were so that you can live as Who You Really Are.

Be reassured that your transition through your past will be graceful and meaningful if you stick with your morning routine. The routine is your solid foundation for stilling the mind and is intended to bring your awareness to your thoughts and how scattered or still they really are.

We will begin by going to the place where most of us reside today: the old paradigm. As we are here in this moment, our fears, our thoughts, our stories are all ready to be invited inward into the Soul of Who We Really Are. Through the unveiling of your stories to yourself, you will see how these stories were written long ago and really have no true significance today. You will find that fears you think are real today, can be caste off in just an instant. But first, we must start with where you are today: still investing in your story.

The following is a story as well. It is a story about your Whole Self. Each of us has four different energetic bodies that make up our Whole Self: the mental, emotional, spiritual, and physical bodies. The four bodies need to be balanced in order for us to live as our Whole Self. Living as your Whole Self is living out the roadmap of your soul. Right now, each of us is more than likely walking around only engaged in one, two, or three of our four bodies. We have forgotten about our soul and all of its innate wisdom. Each one of these bodies plays an important role in our life. If we experience our life only from parts of each body, we are not living from our Whole Self. If we are not living from our Whole Self, then we are not fully awake to the messages of our soul.

Imagine that when we are born, we are like a whole pie. This pie is split into four pieces: the mental, emotional, spiritual, and physical. When we live fully engaged in only one, two, or three of these bodies or pieces of the pie, we identify with only *part* of our Whole Self. As we go through life, we take the lid off of our pie and allow people to take pieces of our pie out of each section. As adults, we reach a point where only pie crumbs remain, sometimes barely even one.

When we cast off parts of ourselves, we weaken ourselves. Many of life's experiences have been cast off, as well, because we felt the experiences had no meaning in our life, when, in fact, they really did. They were experiences in our life that we no longer wanted to claim or admit, so we gave our power away by denying them. As a result, there is very little left for us to give because we have given away our pie pieces throughout our lifetime. When we gave away certain aspects of our Self, we expected to be replenished, yet all too often, we were not. After years of living in survival mode, we lost touch of what we were really living for in the first place. The good news is that our souls are complete and whole, untouched by any of the pie pieces being taken by others.

It is important to remember that it does not serve us to cast off parts of ourselves that we no longer want to remember. The parts of us ("our Selfs") that have been long forgotten or cast aside are all a part of our Whole Self. The reality is that when we came through hard times—loss of a loved one, disappointment, heartbreaks, huge obstacles, or sadness—these experiences created our Whole Being. Compassion comes from having known these challenges. Fully engaged, our heart has the power to heal both ourselves and others. Living as our Whole Self requires that we call back our power from within and call back all of our pie, so we can live fully integrated once again in all of our bodies. Living from our Whole Self requires that we face our fears and invite them inward to the seat of the soul.

To begin, recite the following:

I ask that my pure essence and pure power, that which is rightfully mine, be returned to me to wholeness forever. Please restore and return to me my gifts, talents, strengths, skills, and life essence. I am asking for a full integration of all of my bodies (mental, physical, emotional, and spiritual), so that I may live as my Whole Self on earth now. Blessed Be.

It is time to reclaim your innate power and stop giving it away with each experience.

You can be of service to others without sacrificing your own life force energy; it benefits the whole when you are fully alive. The way that you will experience this feeling of wholeness once again is to really experience each level of your being and to realize that you must do something different from the way you had been doing things before.

By reclaiming our power and all aspects of our Self, we live the Essence of Who We Really Are. When we are fully integrated into our Whole Self, we are more alive and full of life's essence. There is a richness and wisdom that happens when we claim all parts of the self, for the self and all others who cross our path. A healing can take place as we become more engaged, living fully as our Whole Self. We then feel more alive and full of life, while raising our inner vibration to that of Divine Love.

So far, I have shown you what it will look like to connect in with your soul and intuition. I have shown you a morning routine so you can begin stilling your mind and allowing your inner wisdom to rise up. Yet neither of these tools is going to work well if you do not address the distractions being created by your mental mind. Let's journey inward where you can learn to tame the lion of your mental thoughts and become the Master of your Mind once again.

Our Thoughts Are Energy: The Law of Attraction

The entire universe is made up of energy; therefore, we are all energy. What looks like form is really just a mass of energy vibrating at certain frequencies. The Law of Attraction simply states that LIKE VIBRATIONS ATTRACT, meaning that energies that vibrate at the same frequencies attract each other. Quantum physics has been proving this theory for many years.

We all have thoughts about ourselves that we carry around with us. These thoughts are alive. They either vibrate at a high frequency or a low frequency. Envision that your soul and productive thoughts vibrate at a high frequency and your unproductive thoughts vibrate at a low frequency. When you constantly think negative, unproductive thoughts, your natural high vibration begins to get blocked by the low vibrations of your unproductive thoughts. If this happens over a long period of time, dis-ease can manifest in the body because the body is out of sync with its natural, high-frequency vibration.

The good news is that when you think high-vibrational thoughts, you are drawn into a space of high-vibrational feelings. Since your natural essence is a high vibration, every thought that holds a high vibration is in alignment with your Highest Self. The higher your vibration, the more authentic your life becomes.

Based on the Law of Attraction, consciously choosing productive, high-vibrational thoughts attracts to you high-vibrational feelings and experiences. When you feel love, you attract more love into your life. Raising your vibration means becoming illuminated from within. The way to move out of the old paradigm and into the new is to shift all of your unproductive thoughts to productive thoughts. This process can also be seen as shifting all of your low vibrations internally to high vibrations. When you do this consciously, you are awakening to

Who You Really Are. You are living out the roadmap of your soul.

EVERYTHING is energy.

Energy is electromagnetic.

We are energy, therefore, we are electromagnetic.

We are electromagnetic magnets magnetizing into our world EVERYTHING that happens to us.

All life is based on one POWERFUL physics principle:

LIKE VIBRATIONS ATTRACT

A perfect example of how "Like" vibrations attract "Like" vibrations:

Ping a tuning fork in a stadium with 100,000 other tuning forks and only those

that are calibrated exactly like yours will ping back.

The mechanics of attracting events in our life:

Every FEELING has its own vibration, so

we ATTRACT by the way we FEEL.

Feeling Our Thoughts as High and Low Vibrations

Our emotional body is our energy attractor. It is our magnetic rod of co-creation. Whatever we feel internally, we experience in our outer world. Therefore, if we are not happy with what we are experiencing in our outer reality, we need to check in with our emotional body and our feelings. Remember, the goal is to shift our feelings from unsupportive low vibrations to supportive high vibrations. When we desire to co-create a world where our heart's desires come true, we must first look at how our emotional body is being expressed.

Since the Whole Self is a unification of all of our pie pieces, it resonates at a high vibration. In order for us to live as our Whole Self, we must be able to see where our energy is depleted, or resonates at a low vibration. High, fast vibrations are good energies which calibrate at the same frequency as our Divine Essence. They are closest to Who We Really Are, so they *feel* good. Low, slow vibrations are furthest away from Who We Really Are. They bring our natural energy down, so they *feel* bad or out of sync. You can imagine that when we repeat self-defeating, low-frequency words to ourselves or others, it brings our energy level down. We are so used to existing at the lower frequency, that after many years, it actually *feels* natural, BUT IT IS NOT!!!!! It serves our Highest Good to vibrate at a high frequency, which is a vibrational match to our Higher Self.

As I mentioned earlier, when you feel a low vibration, like fear over a length of time, it starts to override your higher vibrations. The good news is that once you decide to shift your vibration from low to high, the high frequencies always dissipate any low frequency. So, if you focus all of your attention on one high-frequency thought, it will naturally override all of your low-frequency thoughts. For example, the thought of "I love myself and all of those around me" will naturally dissipate any thoughts of fear, doubt, worry, or stress. So, it benefits us to stay focused on empowering, high-vibrational thoughts.

Because there is an energetic vibration that each of our thoughts put out, we need to become more conscious of these thoughts. It is time to align your inner high vibrations of Divine Love with your daily thoughts. Since low frequencies are transmuted away by higher vibrations, it is clear that to heal your past and any leftover residue, all you need to do is hold a high vibration: Be Love. All it takes to be love is to choose love.

Our thoughts come from our personality self, not our Divine Self. Living as our Whole Self and following the roadmap of our soul is about reconnecting with our Divine Self, where all thoughts resonate at a high vibration naturally. In any given moment, all we need to do is stop all focus on the small-scale thoughts of our limited-perspective personality self and open up fully to our Whole Self. The way to do this is to stop engaging in any thoughts that do not feel good. Just drop your attention inward to your soul, and feel love anytime that a disempowering thought arises.

The more we stop following the thoughts of the mind and start focusing inward to our Divine Essence, the better off we become. We naturally start to feel more whole, alive, complete, and fulfilled because we are honoring a part of ourselves that we have ignored for so long. The invitation to you always is to stop the mind and drop your stories, as you move inward to your soul. Your soul invites your fears home, and your mind no longer dialogues back and forth about all of its fears. It truly is amazing to awaken consciously to what has always been within us, awaiting our return.

Sometimes, stilling the mind requires we take baby steps, while other times, one big leap is enough. This book shows you both ways. This section continues to show you how to take the baby steps necessary to awaken. First, we must wake-up out of autopilot mode and become conscious of our thoughts. Once we begin observing our thoughts, we can see which hold a low vibration and which hold a high vibration. We then want to release any thoughts that hold a low vibration by NOT engaging in them. When they come up, we must set them free. We must be willing to stop the self-perpetuating cycle of self-sabotage and self-defeat. We are in charge of our thoughts, they are not in charge of us. We have permission to tell our thoughts that we no longer wish for them to run our lives. This is the point of the candle exercise in your morning routine. The candle gazing gives you an idea of how chaotic or still your thoughts really are. If they are all over the place during your candle gazing, keep pulling your attention back to the candle. This practice then allows you to do the same when you are engaged in your day and your mind wants to keep you distracted away from your soul. The power is in your hands to still your mind while simultaneously asking your soul to come forth. It truly is an amazing experience.

As you start to see your thoughts, you can then decide which thoughts are productive to your journey and which ones are not. The key is that the more you engage in thoughts that hold a high vibration, the less the unproductive thoughts stick around. Again, they cannot stick around because high vibrations transmute low vibrations.

According to The Law of Attraction, your inner feelings have a direct correlation to what you are experiencing in your outer world. By consciously choosing empowering and productive thoughts and feelings day-in and day-out, we shift our vibrations into alignment with our Divine Essence. Our soul then replaces all of the old stories of our past that no longer serve us. The result is that we rise above our past stories by literally raising our vibration to one that is in alignment with our Higher Self.

On a practical level, all you ever need to do is ask yourself: "Does this thought come from love or from fear?" Your answer should always be love. When you engage all of your attention on pure productive thoughts, you will see your world shift right before your very eyes. It is time to learn how to rise above your human story and open up to an even greater one. Now let's discover together how you became who you see yourself as today.

First, I want to show you how your thoughts and feelings are creating your current reality. The Law of Attraction shows you how you can create your world from a new perspective. This understanding is important to have as your foundation before you go back into your past. Your past does have a direct correlation with who you think you are today, but it has nothing to do with Who You Really Are. There is a distinct difference that you will learn as we move forward. Just remember as we move through this chapter, in order for you to live your best life, you will need to let go of the self-defeating thoughts of yesterday. Join me, as I show you how.

Limiting Core Beliefs

Our human mind in its original form is intrinsically pure, but others outside of us have projected their software onto the pure hard drive of our mind. Now, it is time to set free all of the software that was injected upon our mind's hard drive, making room for our soul. The true imprint, or hard drive, of Who We Really Are will always reside at the core of our being, our Divine Essence. It is this essence that our mind will want to override.

Our beliefs about our self and our life determine what we say, feel, and do. Many of these beliefs remain on an unconscious level, yet they still dictate how we experience the world. Right now, we all hold thoughts in our minds that are either resonating at a high or a low vibration.

Limiting Core Beliefs are the fundamental judgments that we hold as true today that were placed upon our Self, by our self, at some point in the past. These self-beliefs limit what we reach for, and what we achieve. They are beliefs we hold about ourselves, others, and life's circumstances that have been repeated for so long, they have become ingrained in us, and are difficult to change. They also cause us to block any conflicting (positive) information, while, at the same time, confirming any new negative information. In this chapter, we will focus our attention on the beliefs we currently hold that no longer serve us and learn what we can do to change them.

Our beliefs are the internal stories that we tell ourselves that end up on the front page of the newspaper of our life.

Earth is a realm of duality where all things appear to exist in opposition. Since there appears to be separation between things, the mind backs up this belief with its thought forms. The gift of this book is to help you relieve your mind of separation and open your heart to the union of All That Is.

Each of us adopted different beliefs as we grew up, although not every belief is unproductive. Here, we are just going to focus on the unproductive thoughts about yourself that you hold onto. These thoughts hold a low vibration, covering up your higher-vibrational thoughts authentic to Who You Really Are. These thoughts stem from fear. As children, we were ego-centered. When a situation occurred, we consciously believed that we had "discovered" something true about ourselves.

For example:
You are chosen last to join the team at recess, your mom tells you that you are lazy because you do not clean your room, your friends call you stupid, and even the dog doesn't want to play with you. You then reach a point where you say to yourself, "I got it: I am stupid, lazy, unloved, and unworthy. This must be true because everyone around me is pointing this out with their actions."

As early as childhood, we started giving away our power and ingesting the beliefs, or software, of those outside of ourselves. As this happened, we adopted one of two ways to cope with what we innately felt was not in alignment with our Authentic Self: Person A gave in and adopted all thoughts as their own, while Person B rebelled against these thoughts. Either path is a way of surviving in a world where we were expected to keep up or get lost in the swirl of life.

Another example:
Let's say your parents were very judgmental of you and always put you down. They told you that you were ugly, lazy, no good,

and/or worthless, either through their words or actions. Person A believes these messages as real and adopts them as her truth. She gives in and goes with the flow instead of speaking up for herself. She gets tired of hearing the negativity, so she shuts down her emotions and just follows the lead of others.

Person B, on the other hand, rebels against these statements. In her rebellion, she might become goal-oriented, driven, shut-down emotionally, and equate money and success with love, etc., as her form of rebellion. She shuts down emotionally and pushes everyone out of her way. She does not feel love, and so she seeks unhealthy ways to receive this desired love.

Take a minute to look at whether you are Person A or Person B. If you do not identify with either one, that's ok, too. (Remember that not everything in this book is going to apply to everyone.) If you do identify with Person A or Person B, you either adopted the beliefs imposed upon you and gave in to become a perfectionist and people-pleaser, or you rebelled and shut-down your emotions, turned to some kind of addiction, and became independent, denying you were any of what others said you were. Ironically, both A and B are natural coping mechanisms provided by our minds to help us survive while existing with the amnesia of Who We Really Are.

You see, our mind only knows how to be in survival mode. The only route it takes is via the software that has been placed upon its hard drive, offering the conscious mind only certain paths based only on past experiences. Our mind does not automatically go into our imagination and create a new way of doing things. The only way to co-create the world is to be conscious of what thoughts we want to play out and which ones no longer serve us.

When we engage in thoughts that hold a low vibration, we embrace our personality self ONLY. Likewise, when we engage in thoughts that hold a high vibration, like love, we live from our Divine Essence. The only reason we hold onto thoughts that hold a low vibration is because we are blaming someone or something outside of ourselves. So, to correct that old paradigm mindset, I will remind you that everyone is an actor or actress playing out a part so that you can know your true Divine Self. This means that our entire past has been colored by our own perception of it. Everyone plays out a part in order to give us an opportunity to shed illusion, and embrace Divine Truth.

By releasing our hold on our personality self, we allow our true Divine Self to come forth and shine. In the next exercise, you are going to identify some of your own core limiting beliefs. You will need a pen and paper.

1. I invite you to begin recalling the story of your past. Brainstorm the words by remembering the wounds from your past.

    Who hurt you? What did they tell you? How were you treated? Now begin to look at your life today and the people who surround you. What are the characteristics of others that you cannot stand? Which characteristic is the most painful? What words do you dislike the most to be called? These words should strike a nerve within you that makes you feel a bit uncomfortable. It may even bring you to tears as you recall the experiences, words, and emotions.

2. Write out 3 or 4 core limiting beliefs that you have identified.

    If you are still having trouble identifying your own personal limiting beliefs, this list should help you out: No one can be trusted; everyone is out for themselves; there is not enough to go around; I can only count on myself; I never get a break, the rug will always be pulled out from underneath me; no one cares; bad things always happen; they always need me; life is hard and then you die; I'm unattractive, unworthy, not good enough; I have been abandoned; if it feels good it could be taken away; I'm not worthy of being forgiven; I feel neglected; it's not ok to make a mistake; I can't do that; I'm clumsy; I have a fear of unknown; I'm insecure, unappreciated, a disappointment, a failure, unlikable, isolated, worthless, a screw-up, unlovable, unimportant, incapable, a loser, wrong, needy, betrayed, disposable, insignificant, stupid, and smelly.

3. Keep this list with you as we continue to look at how you have been living your life.

    Remember, this list is just a means to an end. It is time for you to identify what your life has been like as a result of forgetting the roadmap of your soul, so you can begin to heal your past and move forward into the light of Who You Really Are.

The point here is to bring into your conscious mind the stories of your past so you can make conscious choices to set free those thoughts that no longer serve your Highest Good. I want you to see that no matter if you are Person A or Person B, you did what you needed to do given all the resources that you had available to you at that time. Neither is good nor bad, they are just examples of ways that the mind creates a structure in order to survive in this world of fear.

As long as you hold this limiting core belief or similar ones as TRUE, you will spend all of your time and energy "proving" that you are NOT this or that. Ironically, *you* were the one who placed this belief over your Divine Essence in the first place. So, you are the one who needs to let it go and replace it with empowering thoughts, shifting your core beliefs from limiting to productive.

Moving out of limitations and fear and into our Divine Essence is essential in our world today. My intention is to empower you to let go of all your outmoded beliefs and create new patterns of Divine Love. When we identify our limiting core beliefs, we give ourselves permission to let them go and recreate who we want to be now.

Let's continue putting all of the pieces together. In the new paradigm, you no longer have to be unaware of what subconscious thoughts are creating your reality. You can now rewrite your story to play out the way that you desire it to be. In order to do this, you must become aware of the subconscious and conscious payoffs you receive by keeping true to your stories.

Identifying Your Payoffs

To continue inward, let's learn about payoffs. A payoff is some way that we decided, either subconsciously or consciously, that it was ok to behave the way that we did, and something we received as a result of what we did. These payoffs do not serve our Highest Good because they come with hidden agendas, or stray from the root cause of our pain and suffering.

Remember that the last exercise was designed to get you acquainted with the stories from your past that hinder you from living to your fullest potential. This next exercise is intended to help you dissect your story so you can see what personal payoffs you receive by holding onto old beliefs. Once you can see why you are holding on to them, you can instantly set them free.

It is only your mind that wants to convince you that your stories are real. In actuality, they are just a fabric of your life, a tapestry created by the mind to keep you in survival mode.

Becoming aware of your payoffs gives your soul a chance to clear away the pain and hurt you once ingested.

1. Identify the payoffs that you have received from the adoption of each limiting belief and claiming it as your own.

    Below, you will find a list of payoffs that we receive by holding onto our limiting beliefs. Remember that these payoffs are coping mechanisms that have been adopted by you in order to survive in the old paradigm founded on fear. You are bringing these beliefs and payoffs into the light because, now, you are moving into a new paradigm founded on Divine Love. In this new paradigm, there is no room for fear, self-sabotage, or unproductive ways of being. First, write down one of the limiting beliefs identified in the last exercise. If you had a hard time coming up with one, this list should help you. I would like for you to circle all of the payoffs that you think you get when you hold onto your limiting belief:

    a) I get to distract myself from underlying feelings.
    b) It is soothing and lowers my anxiety.
    c) I get sympathy and attention.
    d) I get approval and admiration.
    e) I get a rush.
    f) I get to avoid revealing myself.
    g) I get to avoid being responsible for the state of my life.
    h) I keep people from confronting me or getting angry with me.
    i) I get to be right and make others wrong.
    j) I get to fit in and not threaten anyone.
    k) I get to have a sense of belonging.

l) I get to blame, and avoid looking at my part.
m) I get to feel sorry for myself.
n) I get to convince myself that I am doing something useful.
o) I get to avoid the terror of emptiness.
p) I get to avoid the risk of rejection by never asking others for help.
q) I get to remain in a fantasy world.
r) List any others that come to mind.

2. I would like for you to combine your limiting beliefs with your payoffs to create a story like the following:

    Mom used to leave me at school, and so I felt abandoned. After she did it long enough, I started to feel sorry for myself. So, if mom would abandon me, then I could feel sorry for myself. I adopted the limiting core belief that I am not worthy, or else she would remember me. I carried this core belief with me throughout my relationships with men. If they would not show up, then I could feel sorry for myself. Along the way, I shifted my unworthy feelings into the methods of Person B, and I started to rebel against that belief. I began to separate myself from people and became very independent. I got married as a strong independent woman to my polar opposite: a feminine male. So, I gave myself another excuse to feel sorry for myself because I had to do it all. My payoff was that I got to feel sorry for myself and push people away.

3. Apply your payoff and your limiting belief to the following questions:
    - What do I get from this behavior that, even though it is hurting me in many ways, is hard to give up?

- Can I feel how much this belief is hurting me?
- Do I see how much I have to gain if I set it free?

4. Ask yourself where you are focusing your attention:
   - What fear am I willing to take out of the driver's seat today? What do I need to ask for to make this happen?
   - Am I taking 100 percent responsibility for the quality of my relationships?
   - How can I release my need to be in control today? What actions will I take?
   - How does it feel for me to prioritize self-care over caring for others?
   - What do I notice about my ability (or inability) to receive from others?
   - What feelings have been more difficult to feel, and in what ways have I been avoiding them?
   - Am I an optimist or a pessimist?
   - Why am I so bitter? So angry? Who am I blaming?
   - Am I the buffer or the go-between? Am I the people-pleaser? Do I fix everyone else's problems?
   - Do I have any boundaries?
   - Am I walking around with lots of guilt, always feeling like I will let people down?

All of these questions are intended to make you more aware. I am certain that your stories are not as pretty as you may like them to be. What did you realize about yourself after you noticed what payoffs you were receiving? What stories about yourself are you still telling yourself and others that quite possibly are no longer true?

As children, we incarnated as pure Divine Energy, always resonating at high vibrations. When the software of others was projected upon the clear hard drive of our minds, we adopted it as real so we could manage this world and all that it was constantly throwing at us. Our society taught us many things that went against how we felt inwardly. As time went on, we adopted more limiting beliefs that covered the core of Who We Really Are. In order to keep this cycle up, we needed to unconsciously adopt payoffs so we could make sense of why we were reacting and living the way we were.

The greatest way to heal from our past is to accept it for all that it has taught us about Who We Really Are. You have permission to hate your past, but I invite you to stop hating the people that played out their part so you could know yourself better. Let's continue to put all of the pieces together so that you can move forward in love, setting free your pain.

Self-fulfilling Prophecies

A self-fulfilling prophecy is some idea or belief that you repeat to yourself daily that eventually becomes your reality. Being conscious of our thoughts is the first step on the path to changing them. Each of us has created self-fulfilling prophecies that may currently rule the way we experience our outer world. We consciously or unconsciously create these statements and tell them to ourselves to keep us stuck in our old ways of fear. The following exercise is going to help you to identify some of your own self-fulfilling prophecies.

1. Here are some examples of self fulfilling prophecies:
   If I was told I was lazy, then I never had to prove anything to anyone.
   If men do not show up, then I can feel sorry for myself.
   If I stay depressed, then I do not have to take responsibility for being overweight.
   If I doubt myself, then I do not have to awaken to my Authentic Being.

If I believe that I am not creative, then I do not have to take any risks.

If I get fat, then men do not have to look at me and I can feel safe.

2. Now, write out one self-fulfilling prophecy that you currently tell yourself:

   Use your stories about how your family or friends treated you in the past, as well as looking at your current life stories. Use your list of limiting beliefs and payoffs. Go back, and replay what your family used to say to you: you are fat, you are lazy, you are unworthy, etc. Did one of your family members leave when you were young—did you feel abandoned, neglected, unheard, etc.?

   If_____

   Then_____

The objective of this exercise is to help you bring into your conscious mind what unconscious patterns you are creating. Remember that your thoughts are integral in co-creating your reality. By becoming more aware of where these deep-seated thoughts come from, you can choose to replace them. As you choose to become aware of your self-defeating thoughts, you start to call back your power and live from your Whole Self, once again.

All of us walk around with wounds buried deep inside. While these wounds remain buried, our subconscious minds try to create scenarios where we can live out these inward stories. All too often, we overcompensate because somewhere in our souls we know that the behavior is not authentic. After years of overcompensating for something you are not even conscious of, your soul is trying to tell you that you don't have to have it this way anymore. Instead, you can live from a place of pure love and joy.

For so many years, you have identified yourself as these traits and built your whole personality around them. Underneath all of this, there lies the crystal of your soul, untouched by any of these experiences. The new paradigm asks you to tap into your inner light right now. In order to live from your Authentic Self, you will have to let go of your wounds, pain, and suffering because it was only your mind and your personality self that created these things in the first place. To shift out of the old paradigm, we must be willing to set these unhealthy ways aside for good. Let's move forward where the healing of your wounds will continue to unfold. By letting go of these behaviors, you will return to feeling at peace and be at one with yourself.

Forgiveness

Throughout this book, I have shown you new ways to view your current life. Sometimes it takes an act of courage to try something new. Other times, it may feel like we are taking a risk. Taking a risk is about choosing to leap out into the realm of infinite possibilities, a space from where all dreams come. Taking a risk is to be awakened to your soul's purpose for existing, calling forth the primal energies that are ready to be expressed through your direct experience, thereby moving you out of fear and into love. You display courage when, despite all of your fears, you go into the unknown. Life goes on with a million and one uncertainties, which is its freedom. It is time for us to get out of our own way, let go, and allow our Divine Essence to flow forth.

I bring this up because asking for forgiveness is about choosing to see your life from a new perspective. You may need to ask for courage, strength, and inner power to shift out of your old wounds, or it may be easy for you. Either way, today is a new day for you, where you have the freedom to choose to set your old pent up energies free, or to continue holding onto them.

There is power in forgiveness. This lies in the premise that forgiving those who have hurt us in our life is a gift to us. It means that we are unwilling to be controlled or dominated by this person by keeping the hurt alive with hatred and anger. Forgiveness is the willingness to free our Self and others from the role of the abuser in our life. When we forgive someone, we are not condoning their actions; instead, we are releasing our Self from perpetuating the energetic pattern that has caused pain. In every situation where forgiveness is necessary, there is an abuser and a victim role. We have chosen one or the other of these roles in order to learn a lesson.

The first step of forgiveness is to open up to a new perspective. This new perspective says that everyone on earth is playing out a part for you so that you can learn your life's lessons. It says that on some innate level, the two of you contracted to meet up and play out a particular role for each other. These contracts can get messy at times because we are never conscious of them.

The second step of forgiveness is to forgive yourself. You were not aware when the event or experience occurred, and most likely, you were caused pain and suffering. Hanging onto anger is suffering. Gossiping about another is suffering. Only seeing the experience from your point of view is suffering. This step of forgiveness gives you an opportunity to allow your pent up energies to be released. Remember that in each situation you were either the victim or the abuser. The roles switch all the time. Now you can forgive yourself for each role you have ever played that may have caused you or another any pain. I guarantee you that there is someone alive on this planet that you hurt as much as you are feeling hurt right now. The following exercise is intended to help you get started on your own self- love healing.

I would like for you to sit in front of a mirror. As you look at yourself in the mirror, I would like for you to send yourself love, from your heart. Ask your mirror reflection to send you love back.. Open your heart to receive this love. Feel the love coming full circle back into your heart. Feel this love coming from all around you, into your heart. Allow yourself to cry and release any pent up energies. Allow yourself to receive this love into your body, to heal. Ask your soul to send you love. Look at yourself in the mirror during this exercise. Notice that you are just human. Notice that you are loved—loved by all the legions of Divine Love that surround you. Allow this love in.

The third step to forgiveness is to forgive others. When we forgive, we heal. Whether we are forgiving ourselves or another, forgiveness is a healing that stems from the power of our soul. When we heal, we shift a lower frequency of energy that was attached to our auric field into a higher frequency. Therefore, when we forgive, we are really doing ourselves a favor.

It is time to let go of the pain from the past, and stop fearing pain in your future. There is a great power in forgiveness that allows for the stories of the past to dissipate away and no longer run your life. You set your fears free by facing them head on. Everything happens for a reason. We can see the truth behind any situation when we are willing to forgive.

In the new paradigm, you understand that everyone on earth is an actor or an actress playing out a part so that you can know your true Divine Self. You realize that it is time to forgive those that have made you feel like a victim. Forgiving someone is seeing the experience from a new perspective. The power is within us to see our life from a new light and accept our journey for all that it has taught us. The vastness of being open, with acceptance, will cultivate compassion in your heart, forever replacing the old judgments, pain, and suffering.

Given this different perspective, I would like to share with you the easiest way that I have found to forgive. You can use these three key phrases to forgive yourself, another person, a group of people, or a circumstance. In forgiveness, these three key phrases are powerful: *I'm Sorry—Thank You—I Love You.* ***I'm sorry*** *that I did that to you or you did that to me—****Thank you*** *for teaching me more about Who I Really Am—and* ***I love you*** *for playing your role perfectly so I can know my True Self better.*

When we use these three key phrases and really mean them, we release the negative energetic hold the person has had on our life. I invite you to do an experiment this week and just say these three key phrases over and over again to yourself until they feel authentic. If you have done this work and have no one to forgive in your life, just practice telling yourself, "I Love myself, I love myself, I love myself!"

Now you are going to do an exercise of forgiveness where you can apply what I have just shared with you in your own life.

1. Identify someone in your life whom you are willing to forgive based on how I have described forgiveness. Ask yourself the following questions regarding that person:
   - Do I need to associate with the person triggering this pain right now? If yes, why? If no, why not?
   - When I am triggered by this person, what person from my past does their behavior remind me of? Dad, mom, family members, co-worker, friend, etc.?
   - Am I ready to transmute this wound into a place within me that is whole and complete?
   - Do I have the courage to speak my truth in this situation?

- Am I going to stay in a place of anger and hurt with the wound wide open, or heal it?
- Am I going to move into a place where I am asking for the negative low vibration to be replaced by a positive one?
- Have I asked myself what lesson I need to learn in order to set this energy free and create a new vibration?

    Feel free to recite the following:

    What do I need to understand about why that experience happened? Soul, show me today an area in my life where I am in need of learning so that I may move forward in my life. I am open to receive guidance and clarity in my life. I invite in my soul to guide me with strength and wisdom to understand what lesson I asked to learn from this person or experience. I accept that person for what they have taught me and I set them free. Blessed Be.

2. Next, continue with the mirror exercise:

    Sit in front of your mirror and start by sending yourself love into your heart. Receive this love. Now, send this love to this person you need to forgive.

3. Recite the three key phrases to that individual by visualizing a conversation with them.

    Sorry, Thank You, and I Love You—Sorry that I did ___ to you or you did ___ to me—Thank you for teaching me more about Who I Really Am, and I love you for playing your role out perfectly so I can know my True Self better. I believe that the lesson you have brought into my life is_____.

In order to really live in the new paradigm, it is time to see that everyone in your past, present, and future is an actor or actress playing out a part so you can fulfill your purpose on earth. At some point, you blamed them for their actions, which created a need for you to forgive them in your future. Now that your future is here, it's time to accept the journey for all that it has given you.

When we decide to stop identifying with our thoughts and the pain of our past, we drop our old identity and feel the deep peace of Who We Really Are, instantly. Life is a learning experience. The model of the new paradigm accepts all those who play their parts out perfectly. It is time to view your life from a new perspective and begin to accept your past for all the glory and gifts that it has provided.

Forgiveness is sometimes parallel to putting closure on old relationships that no longer benefit your well being. Let's continue forward, as you learn how to put closure on these types of old relationships.

Putting Closure on Old Relationships

One way to let your old, outmoded thoughts go is to have closure with the memory of what put the thought there in the first place. The memory most likely has a person attached to it in some way or another. In the last chapter, we discussed forgiving this person. In this chapter, we will continue in alignment with setting free the old, pent up energies that kept you from moving forward into the new paradigm.

Closure means that we are willing to set that person or experience free to return again to an original form. It means that we are closing that door so an even better one will open. Closure allows our energy, which is dispersing in a million different directions, to come back to center. Illness and disease are sometimes caused by not having closure in one's life. Closure sets us free.

I would like to point out two different types of closure. The first relates to people in our life whom we need to energetically set free so we can go our separate ways. The second relates to those people in our life who are not intended to leave our lives for good. Instead, the relationship just needs to be seen from a new perspective. I will address the former first.

In situations where we realize that we are shifting and changing while another around us is resonating at a low vibration, it is time to put closure on that relationship. Many of us avoid putting closure on things because we are:

- Holding out hope that the other person will change his or her mind, and everything will go back to the way it used to be.
- Not willing to face the unknown of what will happen when we do let go.
- Enjoying beating ourselves up.
- Unaware of how to put closure on the situation.
- Unaware of where we need to have closure.
- Avoiding confrontation or "rocking the boat."

We can all relate to the existence of relationships that drain us—those that we allow to occur because, inside, we are receiving some kind of payoff for the exchange. Really look at this for a moment. If you choose to set a person like this free, you will be happier. Is this ok with you, or do you like to stay immersed in the drama of chaos and turmoil with someone who drains your high-frequency energy? In order to live in the new paradigm of Divine Love, we must set free the old relationships that hold us back. The following exercise will help you identify if there is anyone in your life with whom you would benefit from having closure.

1. Today, I would like for you to identify where or with whom you need to have closure in your life. Ask yourself:

By holding onto something or someone, how am I held back from living my Divine Essence? Who do I need to set free: a coworker, friend, lover, parent, child, or significant other?

2. Now that you have this person in mind, I am going to take you through a visualization to see how the conversation with this person would unfold before it actually occurs. Visualization is a wonderful way to release a person from your life and to heal. Our minds can be very powerful when we use them for visualizing win/win scenarios. Remember, if it serves your Highest Good, your relationship will shift to a higher level instead of being closed and released.

3. I want you to visualize this person standing in front of you. Now, visualize the conversation in the exact manner that you would like for it to play out. Get into your body and feel how you would like it to feel when you have this conversation. Use your imagination as you design the conversation to go as smoothly and positively as possible.

4. The next thing you are going to do is state your intention:

    For example: My intention is to put closure on this relationship and all relationships and experiences in my life that no longer serve me. Please bring me the clarity, guidance, and strength to show me how to do this easily and gracefully. I ask for the courage to say what I need to say to whomever I need to speak my truth. I envision this to be a win/win situation for everyone.

5. Now, you are going to write out, or continue visualizing in more detail, your true heartfelt feelings about this person.

Visualize or write out your side of the situation. Be clear as to why you see putting closure on this relationship is what you need to do to take care of yourself right now.

As your week unfolds, you will most likely be given an opportunity to play out your visualization, or give this person your letter, putting closure on this relationship that no longer serves your Highest Good. Remember that it is most likely beneficial for both of you to shut the door on your relationship so a new door can open. In this way, you are co-creating your reality. So, when you visualize a loving exchange with a win/win attitude, in both of your Highest Goods, it unfolds in just that manner.

By calling in love and support from your soul and stating that your intention is for closure, you will most likely find that the actual experience unfolds better than you would have imagined. All you need to do is set your intention to be about closure. Honor this person for playing out their role in your life, and set them free to guide someone else.

So many of us avoid closing doors because we fear what the results may be or we do not want to hurt someone else's feelings. If it serves both of your Highest Good to remain friends— just at a new level—it will be.

The second type of closure is where a relationship may need to have closure on a certain level so that it can be reborn onto a new foundation of Divine Love. We must remember that we will never, and should never, try to change anyone. All we need to do is focus on our own self. For example, when we have a family member in our life with whom we do not get along, putting closure on the relationship really means making a conscious decision to do away with the old relationship and choose to see it in a new light. This new way is about returning the focus back to our Self.

For example, this person may be pushing our buttons because we have buttons to push. Subconsciously, they pick up on our buttons and play out a part, thereby offering us an opportunity to do something different. How often do you notice yourself reacting to this person instead of being proactive? This type of closure is about you reclaiming your power and putting closure on all of the wounds and buttons that you allow others to push.

It is not about the other person now, nor will it ever will be. It is about you choosing consciously to see the gifts this person has brought you. This person has graced you by showing you areas in your life that need shifting from within. This form of closure is really about each of us taking our power back by seeing ourselves, and thus our relationships, in a new light. People will no longer continually stress us out, push our buttons, or frustrate us because we are choosing Divine Love.

Today, you have an opportunity to make a HUGE BREAKTHROUGH! You get to choose if you would like to hold on to your inner anger, stress, and frustrations, or if you would like to set them free. I invite you to look at where you are still holding onto your stories from the past. Is there a relationship in your life that you would like to experience in a new way?

I would like for you to visualize this person in front of you and recite the following to yourself:

Dear _____, I appreciate you in my life. You have been pushing my buttons because I placed them there for you to push. Today, I am putting closure on my old wounds and pattern of attracting this low-vibrational energy into my life. I value who you are as a soul and see that from this day forward, we will have a different type of relationship. I can now smile at my inner frustrations and anger. I am shifting this energy by not allowing myself to be a slave to anger and frustration any longer. Today, I put closure on all relationships that have been preventing me from living my Whole Self. Thank you for playing your part out perfectly, as I now see you in a different light.

Life's transitions do not have to be complicated and filled with drama. We can let go of things gracefully and amicably when we choose the higher road. To grow is to have an experience, learn the lesson behind it, and then, set it free. We do not allow ourselves or others to be involved in the highest experience when we remain stuck in the old energies that created the relationship to begin with.

Family members can be amazing people from whom to learn and grow. Many times, our own stuff gets in the way of really seeing the beauty they might bring us. Even if we have a hard time initially seeing the beauty in others, by practicing self-love, we will get there eventually. Putting closure on our past and all of the ways that we have lived our life with blinders on is the way inward. All of our anger, stress, and frustration will dissipate when we choose the higher road of Divine Love. In choosing this road, we are not condoning the actions others have taken; instead, we are allowing ourselves to be set free from being a slave to the memories.

Today is a new day. Choose to set free the bonds of the old and co-create a new life filled with whatever feelings you do wish to manifest. Many of us exist in our minds way too much. Strike a balance today with your mind and your heart. Be willing to set your old ways free and replace them with pure love and joy. Just choose it and it will be.

One Challenge to Moving Forward: Being Tested

Once we affirm that we are going to call our power back, feel empowered once again, and live as our Whole Self, something mysterious happens: We get tested. This is one of the main factors that presents itself as a challenge to moving out of the old and into the new paradigm.

Imagine that one of your lessons is to learn how to stand in your power by speaking your truth. As you declare that this is what you are working on, the universe pulls together opportunities that offer you a chance to speak your truth. Imagine that one day you had a falling out with a long term friendship. Your "friend" yelled at you, creating a situation where she appeared to have power over you. This situation, created by the universe, was your opportunity to stand up for yourself and speak your truth, and it was your "test" to see if you really meant that you wanted to stand in your power. The universe will continue to present opportunities for you to stand in your power until you just do it ONE time.

I promise you that I know how you are feeling when this challenge arises. It appears to be the same old drama, or may even be the same old uncomfortable feeling, so you run from it. Please stop for a moment and realize that I share the idea of challenges with you for a very important reason. Being tested is one of the main causes of what I will refer to as "retreating into the mind." In truth, being tested is really just an opportunity for you to affirm the new you as an empowered, worthy, loving, and compassionate person. All too often when we get tested, we get discouraged because we think that we are going backwards or just not getting it. In actuality, the complete opposite is happening. Just remember that when you affirm to the universe the new you, you will be tested so that you can proclaim this new you through your actions.

Until we get the lesson, we will continue to create situations where people push our buttons so that we can learn and grow. What they are really doing is giving us an opportunity to stand in our graceful power and say *no* to that wound. In doing so, we take the arrow out of our heart, and we become our Whole Self, again.

When situations unfold that may not appear to be pleasant, ask yourself what lesson you are learning right now. You will more then likely notice that this is your chance to move through the lesson, if you do your part. Stop and look at the person in the situation as an actor or actress playing out a part so that you can learn your life lesson and move forward owning your Authentic Self. All of these situations occur so you can release your personality self and live out the roadmap of your soul. This opportunity is a perfect time to ask your soul for guidance, help, and clarity, so that you can see the situation from a new, bigger perspective.

As humans, we like to hold onto the experience, emotions, and thoughts that have caused us pain. But now, times are changing. It is time to bring conscious awareness to the emotions caused by experience, integrate the experience into your present life, and release it and its emotions, so that you can move forward on your journey. Being tested just means that you are willing to fully step out of the old paradigm and into the new paradigm. It shows you that you are an empowered soul. Just remember that the actual test is really just an opportunity for you to own the aspects of yourself that you are affirming as the new you. You are loved.

The words I have spoken to you throughout this book have true meaning if you are willing to put their guidance into action. Recognize either your resistance to, or full acceptance of, what has been shared. Most of all, Divine friend, just live it so that we can collectively shift the energies of this planet more fully into alignment with Who We Really Are, and came here to be.

It is my fullest intention to give you the good, the bad, and the ugly. I wish for you to live fully as your Highest Self. The challenges that arise are created by your soul to help you move forward. Let's continue looking at more ways for you to move into your Divine Essence, by facing any resistance to change that you may have.

Facing Your Self-Doubt and Inner Resistance to Change

Self-doubt is your personality self's best friend. When you remain in a state of doubt, your mind remains in control of what you do and don't get to do. Removing self-doubt is parallel to stilling your mind. Realize that self-doubt is a child of your mind, not your soul. Self-doubt comes up when you are not fully engaged as your Whole Self. For today, tell your mind that you are ready to allow yourself to move with the flow of the healing waters of self-love instead of self-doubt.

To move out of fear, we must face our resistance to change and learn to grow. Fear is only a construct of the mind created to keep us stuck in the drama of our lives, and it exists only because we have cut ourselves off from our infinite source of wholeness. Fear exists only when there are a few pieces of the pie; but when we live as our whole pie, there is no room for fear because all that is exists as Divine Love.

Resistance is born out of fear. This resistance is not real, but only a concept of our mind trying to keep us stuck right where we are. Why? Because it tells us that it is too painful to change. It is happy with only parts of the pie. It knows that if we gather all aspects of our innate power (our pie), we will not buy into the stories (pieces) of the pie. Have you ever been told only one side of a story? Have you ever heard the other side of the story at a later date and were then able to see the experience in a new light? This is how the mind works when we exist as a fraction of the whole. It only feeds us pieces of the whole story, which limits our perspective and leads to fear, resistance, and self-doubt.

The gift is that when we move into, instead of away from, our resistance, we will find that it was only our mind that put fear there in the first place. We must remember to use our hearts and souls to persevere through our perceived roadblocks, so we can live more authentically in Divine Love, instead of with the illusion of fear. All that we ever have to do in any given situation is choose love over fear. The easiest way to do this is to live as our Whole Self. It just takes care of everything. The following will show you how you can face your inner resistance.

1. Let's look at what we can do when we feel this inner resistance come up for us. We can:
   Admit that we are feeling resistance.
   "I feel like closing down and putting this book away."
   Identify why we are feeling resistance.
   "I feel resistance because I never follow through with anything. I am used to being a failure."
   Design a plan to take baby steps to move through our resistance.
   "I will start out by taking baby steps and read this book in sections. I will be patient with myself."
   Ask someone to hold us accountable.
   "Friend, I bought this book for you and me. Would you be willing to go through each section with me and have us hold each other accountable?"
   Identify our purpose behind why we want to move forward.
   "I am ready for a new life. My purpose is to be a better person and live a happier life."

2. Find a sacred, quiet spot (by a tree, on your bed, in nature) where you will not be disturbed.

Today, just sit in stillness and let what has been shared so far, really sink in. Understand the traps of the mind that want to convince you to put this book down and get back to your "to do" list. Be aware of this trap of the mind called your personality. Waking up is a process, and it will take your commitment to really honor this path.

I have written down a vow that I would like for you to embrace. When you are ready, I would like for you to write it out for yourself and sign it. Then, place it somewhere in your sacred space where you can read it every day.

I, _____, vow to live my life from a place of joy and loving creation. I vow to choose thoughts that will create joy and loving creation in each moment. I am 100 percent committed to the full expression of my Whole Self and I call in any and all help I need to fulfill this vow. I am calling back all of my power, my life essence. I vow to listen, trust, and apply my Inner Guidance in every moment. I promise to love myself as I am remembering Who I Really Am. I choose to be filled with joy and Divine Love every time I remember I have taken this vow. I am living fully integrated as my Whole Self now. With every step I take, I am releasing the old paradigm of who I thought I was and awakening more fully to the new paradigm of my Divine Self.

When you can say this vow and really feel its authenticity, you will find that the process of awakening is swift and easy. If you are feeling an inner resistance, go into it. The choice is in your hands: Either journey inward where the magnificence of Who You Really Are awaits your remembrance, or remain where you are.

Chapter Five

Embracing Who You Really Are

Choice is one of our most precious gifts. The ability to choose for ourselves unleashes limitless possibilities for creating a future filled with our dreams and desires and a life free to design and create from our Authentic Self. When we choose to see our lives from new perspectives, we move into the new paradigm of Divine Love.

Each choice that we make, either individually or collectively, alters the direction of our life. Choice is an individual right and freedom that guides us to make decisions about our health, our relationships, our finances, our social life, our lifestyle, and our spiritual beliefs. The quality of our lives is made up of the sum of all of our decisions. All of us have the ability to access our divinity and live from our Highest Good. But, if we are going to live from our highest state of consciousness, we must become aware of the choices we are making in every moment. No one can choose the direction of our lives for us.

Because of the repeated unconscious or unhealthy choices that we each make day after day, we share this space living as parts of the whole pie. The gift is that we each have the power to change our lives and we can choose to do it at any given moment. If we want our lives to be different, all we have to do is make different choices.

To live as Who You Really Are is to continually look within and live from your soul. In the last chapter you noticed how your thoughts create your reality and learned what you can do to change them. Being Who You Really Are means leaving your mind's chaos behind. It means that you must be willing to take a leap into a new foundation of Divine Love. It means that, by now, you are asking your soul for guidance and clarity and are receiving it more fully in your daily life.

The jig is up! The mind is now being revealed for its trickery and the games it likes to play. Do not let the mind overshadow the crystalline structure of Who You Really Are any longer, dearest Divine One. Go forth in the light of pure Divine Love and know that you are loved and honored for choosing to incarnate upon earth. Awaken the lotus of your heart and live your fullest essence here on earth. Together, let's create Heaven here on earth.

Next, we are going to move into clearing out your old limiting beliefs for good. Here, you are encouraged to voice your doubts, fears, negative behavior patterns, or anything else that limits you from becoming your True Self. What you are doing is bringing all of these negative expectations into the open—into the light of conscious awareness—where they are seen for what they really are: an illusion.

Do not look back in anger or forward in fear, but, simply, around in awareness. Your imaginings of fear are far greater than the actual facing of your fears will ever be. When a negative thought arises, let it come up. Label it as fear and let it go.

Clearing Out Your Old Limiting Beliefs for Good

Remember that when we have a low-vibrational thought arise, it serves our Highest Good to set the thought free. When we hear an internal voice that is self-sabotaging, we need to just set it free by not feeding it with our attention. The good news is that it is up to you to let the low-vibrational thoughts go whenever they surface. The bad news is that sometimes the "you" does not want to let them go. Today, I invite you to take a moment before you read any further. Imagine with me, your thoughts as energy—-like clouds in the sky. Your thoughts make up your story, which makes up your personality self, that part of you that accepts limiting beliefs.

Now, imagine with me, that you are watching your thoughts rise up like clouds in the sky. Yet, this time, you just let them pass on by. You see them floating away in a basket, as the wind takes them away forever. In this moment of stillness, your thoughts are just air. They do not dictate who you are or what you are here on this planet to accomplish or play out. Only your soul knows what you are here to do. Only your soul can show you how to listen to your Infinite Wisdom, instead of the stories of your own limiting beliefs.

As children, we knew innately what was real and what was unreal. We tried to speak up, but were shut down time after time. Yes, I know, it did not go over well with us. In order for us to survive in our world, we adopted these beliefs that at some point became limiting to us. At some point, they became our suffering.

Always following the fear-based stories of our mind is practicing suffering. Our soul will always refresh us with its divine grace, love, and beauty. There is nothing we are asked to do in order to keep our soul alive and refreshed, for that is its nature. Our ego, on the other hand, needs to be fed daily, hourly, and in every moment, in order for it to stay alive. Personal suffering continues when we continue to feed our ego. But it is important for our soul that we put our ego to rest during our sleeping hours. When this happens, we wake up refreshed and rejuvenated.

Investigate within: "What am I practicing—-suffering or self love?" If you are practicing suffering, stop feeding your ego and start practicing the art of stilling your rapid thoughts. Be the marvel of your Divine Essence. Imagine with me a day where you wake up and your usual thoughts no longer rule your day. Instead, they are replaced by a calm stillness. You can then focus your mind on what thoughts you want to have.

There really are no obstacles in our lives, except for the ones we put there ourselves, even unconsciously. When we realize that we're the ones who put each and every obstacle in place, then we can remove them, as well. We have the power to heal and dissolve any perceived block that is in the way of happiness. As we remove our mental barriers to happiness, our natural state of being, inner peace, and contentment will follow.

However, if we stay immersed in our self-doubt, fears, suffering, and stories, we will remain in the old paradigm. Our foundation will be made of fear, and we will be stuck listening to our mental thoughts and riding our emotional rollercoaster. Or, we can choose to ride the new wave of our being and choose to let go of our stories. The following is a great dialogue that you can have with yourself when an old limiting belief arises. This dialogue is intended to show you that you have full control of your thoughts and what you want to do with them.

Today, answer the following questions:
- What is my current belief I am clearing today?
- Does it serve me? Why or why not?

- What are the payoffs for holding onto this belief?
- So what—what difference does this make?
- What do I really want for myself?
- How will this benefit me?
- Which is a richer experience: My old belief about me or what I really wish to create?
- What is my New Statement about myself?
- What do I need to ask for to make this transition easier for me?
- What feeling do I need to get into to make this shift?
- How do I feel and how comfortable am I with this statement?
- What is my New Vision for my life?

Here is an example:
What is the old belief I am clearing today?
The belief that I am unworthy.

Does it serve me? Why or why not?
NO, because it only isolates me from others.

What are the payoffs for holding onto this belief?
I get to feel sorry for myself and always be right.

So what—what difference does this make?
None.

What do I really want for myself?
I really want to be loved and be appreciated.

How will this benefit me?
I will feel better about myself and see my worth.

Which is a richer experience, the belief or what I want to create?
The belief that I am important and worthy.

What is my New Statement about myself?
I am supported and nurtured for Who I Really Am.

What do I need to ask for to make this transition easier for me?
I need to ask for support.

What feeling do I need to get into to make this shift?
The feeling of being loved and supported.

How do I feel and how comfortable am I with this statement?
I feel loved and I am about 80 percent comfortable right now.

What is my New Vision for my life?
I am supported, nurtured, and appreciated for my gifts and talents. I see myself as beautiful person who has a lot to offer this world.

Now use one of your limiting core beliefs and go through this list answering each question honestly and openly.

You now have a voice that can be used to shift not only your own consciousness, but the consciousness of this planet. And your voice needs to be heard. You have a lot to share with this world, and the world awaits your arrival. The voice we did not use as children to say *no* when we adopted old paradigm thoughts is the same voice we can use today to say *no, thanks* and set them free from our mind. When old thoughts come up, we can use the above dialogue or tell them: "Thanks for sharing, but I am choosing to listen to my innate wisdom and guidance today."

This phase of awareness and creating a new foundation will take time to integrate fully. As you move into your soul more and more every day, the old ways will simply dissipate. All of these tools, when applied, will transport you out of the old and into the new paradigm.

Replacing Your Self-Defeating Thoughts with Empowering Ones

Now that you are taking responsibility for your thoughts, it is time to replace your self-defeating views with empowering ones. You will be creating "I AM" affirmations and positive statements that will redirect your mind when it decides to follow the old groove of negative thoughts. You will be literally retraining your thoughts to follow a new track in your brain, rather than following the path of the old self-destructive one.

You have looked at your emotional body and how your feelings hold vibrations that are directly linked to how you are experiencing your reality. Now you can become co-creator of your world by consciously deciding what mental thoughts you want to feed and which ones are outmoded and need to be transmuted away.

The best way to be a direct co-creator of your reality is to create positive "I AM" statements that you have learned to use in your daily morning routine. The following exercise will show you how to create new, positive affirmations that you will use to replace your old self-defeating thoughts.

Creating Clear "I AM" Affirmations:

1. Stating "I AM" affirmations is being conscious of your "I AM" Self and bringing the natural state of your Divine Essence forth.

2. The more specific and positive your "I AM" statements, the more you will reawaken the positive that is always within and be able to bring it forth into your life.

3. You are releasing the old core belief system that has been preconditioned within you.

4. This process takes time to shift the unconscious statement of limiting beliefs to the conscious creation of empowering statements.

5. Be Positive, Specific and Simple in creating your affirmations.

6. In the affirmation, do not mention the negative mind set that you are releasing. For example, if your disenabling belief is: "I am worried that I will not be able to pay my bills," do not replace with: "I am not worried."

Now, write out ten "I AM" affirmations that are related to the self-fulfilling prophecy that you are releasing.

For example:
I am open to receiving new friends into my life.
I am eating healthier every day.
I am open to seeing my life from new perspectives.
I am choosing empowering thoughts to say to myself every day.
I am 100 percent committed to living my Authentic Self.
I AM_____

Now write these affirmations out on an index card.

Place these cards throughout your house, at work, or in your car where you can see them. State these affirmations out loud daily, and pay attention to the feeling associated with the positive affirmation. As you begin to shift your thoughts from negative to positive, you will feel your inner vibrations shift as well.

Continue to drop your attention into your body when you state these affirmations so that you can re-familiarize yourself with your pure state of being.

Our "I AM" self is universal wisdom, love, and truth made manifest. It is the indwelling God at the core of our being. The "I AM" self is our individual Divine Consciousness where our every thought, combined with our emotions, co-creates our reality. By creating your own "I AM" affirmations, you direct the energy of your thoughts to be in alignment with your truest desires. Let's continue as you take a look at what your truest desires really are.

Identifying What You Do Want

This next section is about identifying what it is that you really do want. Normally, as humans, we spend 99 percent of our energy focused on what we do not like in life and 1 percent of our energy on what we do like. By reversing that statistic, we reconnect with what we really want and then, bring it into manifestation. When we place our attention within, on loving our Self, we find that everything else in our world falls into place.

The following are guidelines for becoming more conscious about creating your reality:

- What we focus on is what we get.
- All negative emotions come from our past. Therefore, BE PRESENT.
- We always have choices—if something doesn't work for us, choose anew.
- We attract according to how we are feeling.
- Intentional creation is the purposeful directing of our pure, positive vibrations.
- Whatever we feel, the universe delivers.
- Switching from negative to positive thoughts is the key.
- Let the universe take care of the "HOW TO's."
- Trust and enjoy the process.
- Our natural essence is a high vibration.

The following is an example of how you can direct your thoughts in every moment:

1. Identify what you do NOT want—give this only 1 percent of your energy.

2. Identify what you DO want—give this 99 percent of your attention.

3. Drop into the emotion of your desire.

4. Let go, and allow what is in your Highest Good to happen.

For example:
Identify what you do NOT want—give this only 1 percent of your energy.
I do not want to feel unworthy.
Identify what you DO want—give this 99 percent of your attention.
I do want to feel loved.
Drop into the emotion of your desire.
I recall the emotion of when I felt loved in my past.
Let go, and allow what is in your Highest Good to happen.
I am letting go and trusting the process.

Ask for what you want and be willing and open to receive it. Be willing to try out something new to bring it forth. Align your inner vibration with your desires. Plant the seeds of your dreams. Remain focused on them. Let go, and be unattached to the outcome.

In the following exercise, you are going to imagine what your ideal life could look like. This exercise is intended to move you outside the comfort zone of your mind and into your imagination. It is important to dream big. When we dream big, we open up to the roadmap of our soul, allowing our Abundant Self to come forth and be experienced.

You are going to write a paper on your ideal life. The purpose of this paper is to open up your creativity and imagination. Only write down what you do want. Include a collage of pictures if this helps you visualize your ideal life. Expand your horizons to see how grand and magnificent you can dream your world to be. You can use specifics such as actual conversations you have had or are having with loved ones. There is no right or wrong way to do this exercise; it is intended to give your inner child a chance to dream big again. It is also intended to allow you to begin to create a visual of what you are asking for in your life. As you write your paper, get into the feeling place of your dreams. How does it feel to have what you desire and deserve?

Use the next couple of weeks to write this paper in your own way. Process with it and allow it to awaken within you whatever serves your Highest Good. Allow your inner voice to have space to dream big. Design your life the way that you imagine it to be.

Putting Yourself First

Putting yourself first means that you are willing to listen to your own gut feelings and act upon them over anyone else's needs and desires. This is not a selfish act—quite the opposite. It is an act of self-love because you are replenishing your reserves, so you have plenty to hand out to others when the time comes. How often have you done things in your life to please others (family, friends, and coworkers) even though inside you felt like doing things differently? Have you ever continued to say *yes* to doing things even though you wanted to say *no*?

1. Ask yourself the following:
    - Am I making decisions about my life based on what others might think about me?
    - Do I constantly feel like I have to do it all myself?
    - Am I going above and beyond my call of duty just to please others?

- How much of my time and energy is invested outside of myself?
- Am I willing to put my needs and feelings first, even though I may fear confrontation or rocking the boat?

2. I want you to find examples of how you sacrifice your well-being just because you think it will please others.

    How am I pleasing others while sacrificing my own feelings or thoughts in the matter?

3. Write down at least two examples in an If... then ... statement.

    Now, look at these behaviors.

4. Write next to each one what you are getting as a payoff.

    For example:

    If I just do what they say, then I get to avoid confrontation with them.

    Payoff: *avoidance.*

    If I pay attention to what others want me to do, then I won't rock the boat.

    Payoff: *no confrontation.*

    If I pretend that I don't care, then this will just pass.

    Payoff: *Don't have to be honest.*

    (Go back to your own list of payoffs and If ... Then... statements if you need ideas.)

5. Once you have your payoff, I invite you to write out what feeling you would rather have: peace, love, comfort, sustainability, etc.

    Once you have identified the feeling that you are willing to feel inwardly, it is time to get into the emotion of that feeling.

6. It may also help to recite the following:
   Divine Higher Self,
   I am willing to take care of myself first and foremost. Please give me the courage to let go of my beliefs wrapped around this new wave of being. I intend to live from my Authentic Self, which lives from a place of pure Love and Light. Please replace my old habit with one that is empowering and beneficial for All That Is.

Your intuition or "gut feeling" is always right. It has encoded upon it exactly what you are asked to do in any given moment. So often we deny our innate desires because we think we are going to please others by doing what they want us to do. Instead, we deplete our energy by giving it away. Each time you give to others without being fully intact energetically in all of your bodies, you are doing a disservice to yourself and to others. How are you going to be able to give to others when you have no energy reserves for your own well-being? When we learn how to stand in our own power, we get challenged.

People show up as naysayers and act as if we should do exactly what they want us to do. Whose life is it anyway? Remember, everyone around us is just playing out a part so that we can know our Self better. If we feel inside that we need to go right, but everyone else tells us to go left—what do we do? When we listen only with our mind, we get confused and settle for whatever others want us to do. However, if we listen innately to our guidance, we are shown which path serves our Highest Good. Nobody knows better than YOU which road to walk.

First, you must start by accepting that you have your own unique path to walk this lifetime. No one knows what serves your Highest Good better than your own innate or Authentic Self. For today, open up to the realm of the new paradigm, where your energy is infinite because you put yourself first. When you do this, you realize that what you are really doing is standing in your power and being an empowered soul. Your guidance will always create win-win situations for everyone. Today, let your soul win over. Vow to live the Highest Divine Essence of Who You Really Are from this moment forward.

You must focus your energies inward toward replenishing your lost reserves, so you will be a Whole Self or Being, able to give effortlessly to others. It is time for you to make a choice: Give your energy away and have nothing left for yourself, or replenish your reserves and have your cup running over continuously. When you step forward with courage, you will easily transition from a story of pain and suffering into a successful life of peace and joy.

An Empowered Being Has Self-Value
Being empowered means that we are willing to experience life from a foundation of joy, peace, love, and creativity. Being empowered means that we are able to stand up firmly with our new set of beliefs, as we gracefully shed the old ones. Being empowered means that we are focused on power from within instead of power over.

There is a challenge to becoming an Empowered Being. This challenge is that your mind is used to being in control and guiding your every move. We were born an Empowered Being and have just lost sight of this natural state. Becoming empowered is a challenge to the mental constructs of the mind because it is foreign to the way the mind works. The good news, however, is that becoming empowered is familiar to our soul. Our soul knows what it feels like for us to stand in the pure foundation of our Divine Essence.

As we do this work of unraveling the old, setting it free, and embracing the new, our mind will fight back. We will be asked to stand in our power and, so, will be tested. Once we decide that we no longer want to be a victim and are ready to be responsible for our actions, we will be asked to affirm this to our environment. Once we do this, people will come into our life and be naysayers and challenge our new statements.

For example: You have a pattern of being a rescuer and are always putting others first, to your own detriment. As an Empowered Being, you state that you are putting yourself first. That very day, three people call you up and say they need you. The old you would drop everything and do anything for them. The new empowered you will stand in your power and let them know that you are taking care of yourself right now. You will let them know that you love them, but you need to take some time for yourself right now. In this way, you stand in your power, as an empowered soul. You were tested and you passed because you re-affirmed your initial intention. Being empowered means that you see the value that you have to offer this world. It is easy for us to follow the self-sabotaging thoughts of our mind when we have not found our own unique value and purpose. Today is the day for you to claim your self-worth and your value, and shout it out loud to the world. The following exercise will help you redefine your own self-value.

1. Create a list of ways that you DO NOT see that you add value to this world. Look at how you are not living from a place of empowerment.

2. While looking at your list, create a new one that shows at least ten ways that you DO see that you add value to this world, as well as live from a place of empowerment.

    For Example: I am always late, I am stubborn, I am unworthy, or I am controlling.

Now create a new one:
I am compassionate, I am a caregiver, I respect people, I am peaceful, or I am empowered.

3. NOW, look to see if there are any contradictions. Did you say you are controlling but also say you are laid back? If you find that some of your statements contradict one another, pay attention to how you do add value and live from a place of empowerment. I want you to ask at least ten people what qualities they possess that makes them feel unique, special, loved, or empowered to be themselves.

4. Now, I want you to look over this friends list, and find ten qualities that you feel you possess.

5. Next, from the same list, find five qualities that you would like to possess.

6. Now, take the five qualities you would like to possess and write out what keeps you from having them as your own. What belief do you have that keeps you from being this way, as well?

7. Next to the five qualities and reasons you do not possess them, I want you to write out what it would look like to you if you did possess these qualities.

8. Now that you have a vision of what it would look like to have these qualities, I want you to identify how you feel when you look at each one. Then, get into the feeling place of one quality at a time. Drop your attention into your body and really feel this emotion. Focus your energies on that quality until it becomes Who You Really Are.

9. Practice living this value everyday until you feel it is authentic.

Revel in the positives that you feel you possess. These positives are yours to own as the unique talents, gifts, and strengths that arise from your presence, which adds value to this earth.

Even if you had a hard time with this exercise, be kind to yourself. Each one of us has value to add to this world. It no longer serves any of us to think less of ourselves than what we are really here to express. You are a magnificent, magical being, who adds value to my life just because you're reading this book. When you continually feed yourself positive energy, then you create a supportive internal environment in which your soul can grow.

Today, your guidance is to find your personal value and love of self. Ask yourself, "Do I love myself?" What is your answer? When you can easily answer with a *yes*, you will have arrived back home to the truth of Who You Really Are. If you have a hard time answering *yes*, the easiest thing to do is to choose to love yourself anyway.

There is no one who is going to love you more fully, more amazingly, more completely than your own Authentic Self. You have legions of love and support all around you on the unseen realm of life. All you need to do is ask to feel this Divine Love in your heart and it will be there. Put this book down, and get in touch with your heart. Ask your Higher Self to pour golden pure love into your heart in this very moment. Feel this love. Invite it in. Be still until you feel it.

Now that you have felt this powerful love, you can choose to be this love in every moment. Your entire life can shift into alignment with this Divine Love if you choose it. Your mind will try to convince you to stay in your fears. Challenge your mind and take back your innate power. You are a Divine Child of Light—-own this, and live it now.

As you step more fully into your inner power, seeing your personal value and self-worth, you will begin to feel your divine purpose rise up to meet you. You will feel that unique dance, called purpose, which shines within your heart. We were all born with a divine purpose that is imprinted on our cellular structure. Right now, it is buried deep within us, covered by the dust clouds of illusion. Today, it is in your Highest Good to reconnect with purpose.

Finding PURPOSE behind what we do is the true power within each of us. You can start by reconnecting with your daily purpose and eventually reconnect with your inner purpose for incarnating. Being in alignment with our purpose will motivate us to do what we are here on earth to do.

Tonight, you are asked to journal. By journaling before you go to sleep, you release all of the garbage you've collected in your mind throughout the day, onto the paper. Place your "to do" list into your journal, and let it go. Let go of your worries, your stress, and any resistance to change onto which you may still hold. Let this be the beginning of a new vision of your Highest Self. Share your thoughts about your inner purpose and what you think it might be. What are the themes of your life? Ask your soul for guidance and clarity around your own roadmap and purpose for being on earth.

So many times we jokingly ask God what our life's purpose is without really expecting to get a real answer. This time, ask so that you may receive. Ask your soul and be open to receive what it has to share with you. It may come clearly to you that day or it may take years to unveil itself. For me, it has always centered around helping others, but it has just taken on different titles over the years. Be patient with the unfolding of your life's purpose. Just know that every day you can set an intention that has an innate purpose associated with it.

Chapter Six

Responsibility/Self-Care

Rethink ...
how you treat others and make new choices based on
how you would love to be treated.

Reconnect ...
with the awareness that everyone views life
from a different perspective.

Relocate ...
from the old world model into the new world model of
living from your Highest Self.

Responsibility is the ability and willingness of a person and or group to take ownership for the beliefs, thoughts, emotions, behaviors, and choices they have made or are making. The amount of responsibility we assume for what happens to us in our lives is something that we decide for ourselves and it is something that we can change. We tend to take responsibility for those parts of our lives where we feel successful and do not own those parts where we feel we have failed.

The following will give you a good example of what we look like when we move from not taking responsibility for our life to owning our part in it 100 percent:

- *I am at the mercy of my environment. Things happen to me and around me but I am unwilling or unable to see my part in the cause. How could this happen to me? Why me?*
- *I begin to notice that when things happen to me, the one constant is that I am always around. Maybe I am not sure what or how I am involved, but I begin to see some type of connection between me and what is happening to me. I was there, but so was this other person. I did it, but if "so and so" wasn't there, it wouldn't have happened.*
- *I am responsible for everything I do and say.*
- *I am responsible for everything that happens to me.*
- *I am responsible, not only for myself, but to those with whom I have a personal or professional relationship, including what happens to them and my role in it.*
- *I am responsible for the "product/outcome" of the groups of which I am a member and which I facilitate, be it family and children, organizations, culture, etc.*
- *I am personally responsible for my own growth and change, in addition to the directions that change takes and what happens to me. Despite my belief in this, life holds me responsible. I am also responsible for those persons and things within my community. I choose the level to which I accept this.*

Being responsible means we are willing to accept that we create our reality. There is no one to blame because everyone is playing out their part in the play of our life. The pain and hurt from our past can be healed by accepting the journey for what it is.

In the spirit of life, it is time to find out what works for us. If it works, we should own it and stay with it. If it no longer works for us, it is time to try something new. Because we can change our thinking, we can change our life. To change our way of thinking we must be willing to step outside our comfort zone. When we take a deep breath and exist in the moment, we are free to take that extra step into the unfamiliar.

Retreat into the temple of your core, and rest there. This is a time to redefine your truth. Now is the time to cut back and prune away what is not truthful, what is illusion. By doing what is uncomfortable, we can understand ourselves better and grow more fully into our fullest potential. Living as only part of our Whole Self has become comfortable and familiar, but it is not our true nature. We must become more conscious of the choices we make, now, so we understand more profoundly how each of our choices can alter our lives.

Being Responsible by Practicing Self-Care

Being embodied in the physical is a jeweled treasure. Really being in our body is essential to living Heaven here on earth in the new paradigm. Unfortunately, many of us are walking around totally checked-out of our physical bodies. Checking back into our bodies is essential to really living while here on earth. Many of us checked out during our childhood years so we could survive in our environments. Maybe you were made fun of, abused physically, were seriously ill, or told you were too emotional—all great indicators that you may have checked out of your physical body years ago.

Today, check in with your physical body to see if this is true. Are you fully engaged in your physical body? Do you like to engage in your physical body through exercise, movement, sex, play, or fun? Or do you just walk around on autopilot, out of touch with your physical body?

No matter how or why we checked out, today is a new day to get reacquainted with our physical body and apply self-care in our lives once again. Today, we can check back in by being present in all of our body. The physical body is an incredible creation of energy. In order for us to move forward on our path, we must live grounded in our bodies. Now is the time for you to check back in with your physical body, the temple of your soul.

The following exercises demonstrate many ways to get back in touch with our bodies. Although many of these exercises use physical activity, you can also visualize any of these events and you will have similar results.

This phase of returning inward is about us making the time to take care of ourselves. It is about us realizing that in order for us to live out our life's purpose, we must be aware of our physical body, no matter what shape it may be in.

1. Set Up an Exercise Regimen

The first step in starting to bring health into your life is to recognize the importance of taking care of your body. The key to getting started is making a commitment to the idea of improving your health. No matter what your reason for exercising and becoming fit, designing an appropriate exercise program will help you with your commitment and will give structure to your plan to improve your health. Whatever motivates you to exercise is a good reason to start.

A healthy body/ mind/spirit connection is where the spirit is allowed to be expressed. When the body is forced to remain out of balance for long periods of time (called stress), then the physical body is affected and begins to shut down. Humans possess millions of coping mechanisms, utilized on a daily level, both physiologically and mentally, to survive. The overall health of an individual is a component of many things in a holistic approach to life, such as lifestyle, activity level, rest, loving relationships, exercise, balanced diet, empowering beliefs, self-esteem, authentic personality, and freedom from self-hindering patterns. The body/mind/spirit connection is the link to the mental thoughts affecting the emotional realm that, in turn, is played out in the physical body through health or disease.

Look through the following list and see how many of these benefits sound attractive to you. If you can find even one benefit on this list, you have enough reason to begin an exercise program and begin taking steps to take care of your health.

Regular physical exercise will:
- Lower or help control your blood pressure (both systolic and diastolic).
- Reduce total cholesterol, including lowering LDL (the bad type of cholesterol) and increasing HDL (the good type of cholesterol).
- Improve the functioning of your immune system.
- Help you to maintain an independent lifestyle.
- Improve your self-esteem and confidence, and alleviate depression.
- Help you relax.
- Improve your overall quality of life.
- Teach you about goal-setting and dedication.
- Help to relieve and prevent migraine headache attacks.
- Give you a break from daily routines and worries.

Call a friend and invite them to start this exercise routine with you.

2. Attend a Yoga Class
Yoga, a combination of exercise and meditation rooted in Hindu religious practices, is one of the most ancient cultural

heritages of India. It has been practiced in Eastern cultures for about 5,000 years and has fairly recently been popularized in Western society. The word yoga in Sanskrit means "to unite," as in joining the mind and body into a single harmonious unit. The purpose of yoga is to create strength, awareness, and harmony in both the mind and body.

Yoga exercises focus on non-tiring physical activities that bring about poise of body and mind, and have a strengthening effect on the nervous system. Yoga takes care of every little part of the anatomy, and yogic practices are noncompetitive and process-oriented; they provide limitless possibilities for growth in self-awareness, where effort is minimized in a relaxed manner. If you are into meditative practices, Hatha and Kundalini Yoga are good choices. Ashtanga and Iyengar are more intense physical practices and Bikram is good if you are looking for hot yoga. There are many different styles of yoga, so explore until you find the perfect fit for you.

3. Bathe Yourself in Music

Bathing in music refreshes the spirit. It awakens a passion for life that goes beyond the constraints of the mind. Music helps counteract apprehension and fear, enables the exploration of personal feelings, and positively changes mood. Remarkably, music has been found to induce problem-solving capabilities and resolve conflict for the listener. Music invites the mind to be still so that inner joy can be felt.

    a. Purchase a piece of music without lyrics (recommendation Pachelbel: *In The Garden* or Snatam Kaur: *Grace*). Pick something that resonates with your inner rhythm. Listen whole-heartedly. Feel the rhythm and the melody. Absorb all of it. Feel a tremendous amount of joy rise up from within, and allow it to create a deep silence. Be aroused from a place that has been dormant for too long. Believe that this music was orchestrated just for you.

   b. Listen to a song from your favorite CD. While you are listening to the music, begin writing. Begin writing without judgment, criticism, or editing your words. Writing with music frees your mind of chatter, and only then can you hear your inner message. Pose a question about which you are interested in receiving clarity. If the music has lyrics, write a line from the lyrics, and then begin writing the answer to your question. If the music does not have lyrics, create an image that goes with the music, and start writing. Put into action the guidance you receive. Music holds no boundaries.

Music is meditation, and meditation is music. Music starts your heart beating in tune with the universe. Music naturally opens doors that have been closed to you for a long time. Like a breeze passing through you, music clears away the applied concepts of the mind, leaving your soul naked and clear. Music guides you into the heart: the seat of your soul.

4. Read for Twenty Minutes Every Day

Books are messengers, portals of knowledge written down. Books are created by inspiration, motivation, passion, spontaneity, and love. To open a book is to open the floodgates of creativity in your life. A child's imagination is set free when she is read to. It is important to keep the magic of reading alive throughout your life.

   a. Go into a bookstore. Let your heart guide you to a book. Open the book and read what you feel led to read by your Higher Self. Place the book down, and reflect upon what you read. Do this exercise with three other books throughout the store. Be open to the symbolic way that stories and images reveal a bigger picture. What theme ran through all the books? What types of books were you drawn to? What one message did you receive that surprised you? Where did the words take you? What sensations did you feel?

b. How will you apply your bookstore experience to your daily life? Openness is key to integrating this experience. Trust that there is a reason why you were led to particular pages within each book. Your inner-knowing has your best interest at heart. Read with an openness to receive a new outlook on life. Explore through reading about areas of interest you have been hiding from your conscious self. Become educated on a subject about which you know nothing.

c. Read a book and cry with it. Read a book and laugh with it. Read a book that was created into a movie. Read a book that is not a bestseller. Read out loud. Read a book that you would not normally read. Read a book to a child. Reading allows your inner being to come alive.

5. Be Still

Your body is the vehicle for your God Self, your absolute self, to be lived. There is a vibrant energy inherent in all you experience. Be still, and know the kernel inside you that is God.

Read this poem, and reflect upon it every morning for one week:

Be still
Just be
Do not engage in any thought
Be quiet, do not think, and do not make effort
Peace is beyond thought and effort
Keeping quiet is the storehouse of love and peace
Let go
After letting go of the object, do not hold to the subject
The purpose of life is to know who you are
The past is the past; do not carry it on your back
Just simply be still

Reflect on the poem, and recognize it as a discipline of being present in your life. Practice being still and silent, and your spirit will awaken and breathe freely once again. Feel what is innate within you. Shine like a star, and be the star. Stand tall like the tree, and you are the tree. Fly high like the bird, you are the bird. Flow gently like the stream, you are the stream. Be still like the mountain, you are the mountain. You are the universe, and the universe is you. Rest, reflect inward, and be still.

6. Get a Massage

Whether seeking relief for a medical condition, searching for a method to help deal with the stresses of daily life, or wanting to maintain good health, more and more individuals are turning to therapeutic massage. Therapeutic massage involves the manipulation of the soft tissue structures of the body to prevent and alleviate pain, discomfort, and stress, and to promote health and wellness. Massage therapy improves functioning of the circulatory, lymphatic, muscular, skeletal, and nervous systems, and may improve the rate at which the body recovers from injury and illness.

Massage brings about physical, mental, and emotional changes. While the benefits can vary from individual to individual, the following include some of them:
- Boosts the immune system
- Fosters a feeling of well-being
- Reduces levels of anxiety
- Increases awareness of mind-body connection
- Helps relieve muscle tension and stiffness
- Fosters faster healing of strained muscles and sprained ligaments, reduces pain and swelling, reduces formation of excessive scar tissue
- Provides greater joint flexibility and range of motion
- Promotes deeper and easier breathing
- Improves circulation of blood and movement of lymph fluids
- Reduces blood pressure
- Fosters peace of mind
- Helps relieve mental stress
- Enhances capacity for calm thinking and creativity

Massage is a powerful way to live from your authentic being because it alleviates any energetic blocks through therapeutic touch. Massage honors the relationship between body, mind, and spirit, and brings forth the inner healer. Love yourself enough to treat yourself to a massage this week.

7. Go for a Nature Hike

Go forth into the light of things, and let nature be your teacher. Nature has the innate quality of profound exuberance that warms the soul. All of life is interdependent. Nature will teach you this. Bring this awareness into your every moment. Today find a local park that has at least one tree in it. When you find this tree, do the following:

a. Go put your arms around it and commune with the energies of the tree. Befriend this tree. You are never alone when you realize that the tree you are hugging is made up of the same universal energies that you are. Today, you have taken a step and hugged a tree. Tomorrow, go back to the same tree and hug it again. Interestingly, with each day that you hug the tree, you will begin to feel energy moving within you. When you touch the tree, she is as happy as a child. The tree welcomes you even when you are sad. When you give the tree your worries, your sadness will disappear in its presence. You can bring your joy to the tree and she can give you even more joy. You make the tree happy, and it will make you happy. There is interdependence between you two. If you are not truly happy from within, go tell the tree your worries, but only tell them once. The tree has no rules, just know that for you to let go of the stories of your past that keep you from moving on, you must give yourself permission to stop after you let them out. The tree has compassion for you, but it is not attached. It knows only pure love.

b. Sit or stand against this tree. Imagine a pillar of white light 1,000 feet above the tree, streaming through the trunk and down into the core of the earth. Now imagine this same pure light flowing through you, as part of the tree. As part of something bigger, you are grounded by the light and are able to release the mental chatter. Be with no thought, only light, even just for a moment. Think of a single question about which you would like to receive clarity. Pose this question internally to your heart. Look around for something that looks or feels brighter than anything else. Rest your eyes upon it. Do not engage in thought. Allow the stream of consciousness to flow through you. What impressions, sensations, feelings, or images do you receive? These are a symbolic answer to the question you posed. You asked, and you received. Trust the guidance you receive. Weigh it against your heart. It should feel light, loving, and positive.

Be silent by choice. Exist where even a thought is too loud. In order to live as our Whole Self, we need to be fully in our physical body. Ask yourself, "What action do I need to take to really be in my body?" Pay attention to what shows up for you this week.

In nature, walk around and find a flower to smell. Stand close and smell the fragrance of the flower. Start to walk away from the fragrance slowly. Stop when you reach a spot where you cannot sense the fragrance. Move into the scent again. The flower has gifted you with a reminder once again of the interdependence of life. You inhale the oxygen that was given to you from the flower, as the favor is returned through the grace of your exhalation. Be love. Love. Love. Love.

8. Swim or Shower or Place the Sound of Water in Your Home or Workspace

Ninety percent of the body is composed of water—that's remarkable! Submerging in water is bathing the soul in its very essence. Swimming, showering, or listening to water falling upon the earth quiets the mind through living meditation. Play in the water of creation, and allow it to reveal the inner frequency of pure love that lies within you.

This week, engage mentally or physically in one of the following:

a. Swim freely in a pool of water. Allow the water to embrace you in its arms of pure grace. As you swim, release your fears. Let the water wash away the residue on the emotional body that surrounds your physical form. There is no gravity, no paradigm of pain and suffering. Recognize the free expression of your soul. Be in the moment, as you honor all of life that relies on water for its survival. When you are complete, raise yourself out the water with awareness of this experience. Choose to leave your concerns behind. Do not drape them back onto your cleansed body.

b. Shower as if under a waterfall. Imagine the water falling over all layers of your being, washing away what no longer benefits you. The water flows from head to toe, vibrating with internal cells, calling forth wellness. Sing out loud, and open up your channels of creativity.

c. Bring the message of water into your workspace. Each trickle of water invites you to be one with the moment. If the moment serves you well, be with it. If you are not at peace in this moment, act. The sound of water reminds us, even amongst the created noise of the day, that there is inner rhythm to all of existence. Be centered and aware of the natural rhythm within.

9. Go for a Walk

The art of walking parallels the art of manifesting. Free pent up energies trapped in your mental, emotional, and physical body through walking, and open the gate for new energies to flow into your life. Walking is the easiest way to get out of your head and into your heart, creating the life of your dreams.

Choose to stop whatever you are doing, and go for a walk. The mind will want to pull you into all the things you should be doing, but realize what a distraction this is. As you begin the walk, physically listen for your breath. Inhale fully, intent on staying in the moment. Exhale. Let go of today's worries. Unconsciously, you breathe deeper because the mind has relaxed. The energy you normally expend thinking is now being used to stay in the moment. Walk fully aware of where the soles of your feet are guiding you. When you walk with conscious awareness of each step, you are living a walking meditation. Observe sights and sounds. Listen to how the sounds of a city orchestrates into a beautiful composition. If you are in nature, let the pure vibrations of life around you speak to your heart.

Part Three

Living in the New Paradigm

Chapter Seven

Universal Wisdom

- All Forms of Life are Interconnected.
- Feel the Interconnectedness to all of Life.
- Commit Yourself Completely to Liberation this Lifetime.
- I am 100 percent committed to living my Divine Authentic Self.
- Relax and Surrender to Life.
- Let go of the Ego (ALL the past memories attached to the Now).

Principles are natural laws that cannot be broken. The following are a list of twelve universal principles. Each principle summarizes what we've learned in this book. Once you apply these principles in your life, you will live your life in a more accepting and compassionate space. Each principle gives you a better understanding and a new perspective on how to see your life.

The following are ways that you can choose to live your life from a new perspective. Adopt one new universal law a month until you see how it applies to your new lease on life. Be open as you read the following principles because, even if they do not make any sense today, one day they surely will. By being open, you allow your soul to communicate with you new ways of experiencing your current reality. Enjoy.

Principle One: Everybody is Always Doing the Best That They Can

Yes, you have, and always will be, doing the best that you can in any given situation. In your past, you did the best that you knew how, given the resources you had. By accepting this, you move away from any self-sabotaging thoughts that you may have toward yourself.

We can also apply this principle to our family, friends, co-workers, and society. They did the best they knew how, given the wisdom that they had in each situation, as well. Everybody is human and has to learn life lessons in order to fulfill their life's purpose.

Everyone around you is not always going to be going through the same thing, have the same coping mechanisms, or be as aware as you. Yet, we are all in the same position of doing the best that we can. So, by adopting this principle into your life, you begin to accept people around you more fully, and you may even show them a little compassion.

If nothing else, turn the compassion inward to yourself. You are always doing the best that you know how in any given moment. If you don't believe that you are, or need help understanding what compassion looks like, ask your soul to show you. Just set your intention to always be centered in doing your best, and you will be. Blessed Be.

Principle Two: Everyone Gets What They Need Exactly When They Need It

This wise advice will call for us to surrender our attachments to how and when things should show up. Remember that there is a difference between Divine Timing and our ego's idea of when things should happen. When we can see that we will receive everything that we need exactly when we need it, this, too, will set us free from the stress and worries of our life.

Try looking at your life today from the angle of trust. Try something new by trusting that your innate inner being knows exactly what serves your Highest Good. Today, see all those around you as receiving all that they need, exactly when they need it. Be present in the moment. Show gratitude for what has shown up. Treat your desires as if they are already in your life.

Principle Three: There Are No Accidents

Everything really does happen for a reason. There may not always be a logical reason, but there is a greater reason behind why things happen. All "accidents" are just opportunities to grow. Surrender to the grace that there is a higher purpose, even if you cannot see it in that exact moment.

When an "accident" happens, you can inquire within and ask, "What is the purpose or lesson behind why this "accident" happened?" Be open to receive the guidance from your soul throughout the next few days. You may be shown why the accident happened or just learn to accept, for today, that it did happen. But, eventually, you will be shown.

Sometimes there are "accidents" that happen that do not directly involve you, like the death of a loved one caused by a tragic occurrence. I send my love and light to any of you reading this who have lost a loved one in a tragic "accident," and I am here to share with you a larger perspective. If there are no accidents, then, on some level, your loved one did contract to play out that role and transition at that time. There is always a reason behind everything. Innately, within all of us, is our roadmap that has encoded upon it our time to transition. I share this with you in hopes that it will bring you peace. Anything that may appear to be a tragic accident has a bigger purpose behind it. Seen from a higher perspective, all experiences in life are positive.

Principle Four: What You Resist, Will Persist

When we have an inner resistance to something and we buy into the resistance, it will continue to show up until we move into it and through it. A perfect example is when we are invited to an event that would serve our Highest Good to attend. Up until the night of the event, we may feel that it would be a good thing to attend, but our mind feeds us excuses as to why not to go. The night of the event, we feel like it would be fun, but our mind resists us going. So our mind wins over, and we stay home and watch TV.

Whatever lesson we were meant to learn, wisdom to gain, or possible new person to meet was missed because we followed our mind instead of our intuition. It is important to pay attention to our intuition. We are going to be tested and whatever we resist, will persist. So, we might as well face it head on. When we move through our resistance, we come out on the other side feeling amazing. More likely than not, we also gain a new friend, awareness, or sense of accomplishment.

Bring your fears out into the open. They are NOT REAL. Go into your inner resistance, and ask for the courage to move through it, so it dissipates away forever. Any resistance will persist, rising up until you face it, and move through it. Ask your soul to give you the courage to move through any resistance you may have.

Principle Five: We Always Do Exactly What We Want to Do

This one is pretty self-explanatory. We are always doing exactly what we want to be doing. If we want to get up too late to sit and meditate, we will. If we want to stay in a job that we hate, we will. If we want to stay in an unhealthy marriage, we will. There are many reasons why we do what we do. Yet what really matters is our actions: We do what we want to do.

This principle also applies to anyone other than you. They too are doing exactly what they want to be doing. You will never change someone else, so don't even try. Start with your life. Do you like what you see? Do you like doing what you are doing? If not, then do something different. Drive a new way to work, take a class you have been putting off, make a new dish for dinner, call an old friend you haven't spoken to, forgive a family member. Do what you want to do with awareness of why you are doing it and what your intention behind it is.

If you need help doing something different in your life, ask your soul for help. You can change what you do, if you notice that you don't like what you are doing. This is the joy of free will.

Principle Six: There Is No Reality, Only Our Perception of It

No two people ever experience a movie or a television episode or a conversation from the same perspective. There really is no reality, just our perception of it. The reality that we put so much of our fears and worries and stresses into is only based on our own perception of it. Understanding that reality is whatever we perceive it to be is a great way to go through life unattached to the outcome of our journey, and yet fully embracing the moment. When we change our attitude, we will change our life. Be willing to see your life from a new perspective today. Remember the story of the sun.

Principle Seven: Do Not Take Things Personally

When we begin to integrate the above laws, it will be easier to see how we no longer need to take things personally. As we let go of what others think about us, we will begin to realize that we are a magnificent soul, no matter what others project onto us.

All we are asked to start with is the notion that when we let go of the expectations we place upon ourselves, then, naturally, our authenticity will come up. When this happens, we no longer have the buttons or old wounds for others to push. As we teach people how to treat us, we will show others that we are empowered individuals filled with self-love.

You only take things personally when you are not empowered and are confused as to Who You Really Are. Become empowered today, and the rest will take care of itself. I promise!!!

Principle Eight: Be Unattached to the Outcome

No matter what is going on in our life, it is important to be unattached to the outcome. We must dream big, ask for what we want, set our intentions, visualize our desires, AND THEN, let go. When we are unattached energetically to the outcome, we show we trust the process. Remember, what we desire, we already are, and what we seek, we already have. This means that what is in our Highest Good will always manifest for us in Divine Time.

Be unattached to the outcome, so you can free up the energies for the universe to deliver to you exactly what you need. Visualize your intended outcome, let go, and be unattached to how it will manifest.

Principle Nine: We Have All the Time We Need

When we are constantly living in the past or the future, we do not make time to sit down and eat. We do not make time to exercise or go play with the kids. When we are in a state of perpetual motion of the mind, we NEVER believe that there is enough time in a day. Why? Because we are listening to our "to do" list instead of our internal clock. Slow down. Look at today as if you had all the time you need to accomplish everything that actually needs to get done. This perspective will expand your awareness in many different ways. Treat every moment as if there is all the time in the world. Return back to the moment when you feel pulled into your past or thoughts of your future. There is enough. Trust this fully, and watch the magic as your mental concepts of time disappear.

Principle Ten: We Teach People How to Treat Us

People treat us the way that we teach them to treat us. If we do not like the way we are being treated, look within to determine what payoffs we are receiving by being treated that way. If we do not see any, we must create a new pattern and teach people how to treat us with love. Are we treating our Self with love? If so, we should be receiving love in return. If we are not treating ourselves with love, we must change, and then we will see how people start to treat us differently.

Are you holding beliefs about someone that may not be true? If so, you are projecting your stuff onto them, and they are just reacting to your energy. Change your vibration to love, and send this love outward to everyone. You will see the results your heart so desires.

Allow yourself time to integrate these new perspectives into your daily life. Each one of these principles holds a high vibration in alignment with your Divine Essence. Life will continue to bring us perceived challenges that are intended to help us evolve beyond the paradigm of fear. In each moment, all that we are ever asked to do is to be love. In this moment, take time to smile. As you smile, feel the innate joy inside that is waiting to come out and shine. These universal laws are intended to show us how we can live our life in a new way, one created from a place of surrender and Divine Love.

Each of these laws is essential to the future of this world. The old paradigm is outmoded. Today is a new day—a rebirthing. As we are now reawakening, it is time for our souls to rise up, and be experienced. We are here to remember our calling and remind others of Who They Really Are. We are here to remember Who We Really Are, so we can live our best life today.

The heart of my message is to live from a place of love, instead of the old world of fear. All of the war going on in our outer world is a direct reflection of the inner wars going on inside many of us. When we are open to seeing our lives from a new point of view, we adopt a new vibration into our lives. As we vibrate at higher and higher levels, we live more fully as our natural essence. Let's continue looking at ways we can all live our lives more authentically.

Surrendering
- See Everyone Who Has Ever Crossed Your Path as a Benefit to Your Life.
- All are actors and actresses playing out a part so you may know yourself.
- Be Willing to Move into the Unknown—-Ask for Courage.
- Realize You Have a UNIQUE PURPOSE for Being on Earth.

- Choose to Awaken to this Purpose and Live in Alignment with it 100 percent.

To surrender is to let go of what we should be doing in order to allow what is coming forth from deep within us. To surrender is to let go of what was once important to our growth but now is outmoded. To surrender is to discharge our river of separateness into the ocean of Being and lose our resistance and allow what happens to happen.

Let go of:
Going outside of yourself for answers
Excuses
Old ways that no longer serve your Highest Good
Feeling isolated and separate
Trying to figure everything out
Your self-sabotaging thoughts
Your "what if" stories
Your fear of not having enough
Expectations you place upon others
Judging everything as good or bad, right or wrong, black or white

Open up to:
Who You Really Are
Following your innate guidance
Divine Love
Receiving support and unconditional love
Community
Loving yourself daily
Creative ways of living your life
Your personal talents, gifts, and strengths
Trusting the Divine plan
Divine Time

It is our tendency to hold onto things for so many different reasons. The ultimate journey inward requires that we let go, and surrender to the Divine magnificence that is within all of us. The mind cannot conceptualize the capacity of this love; it goes into its databank and tries to figure out what it can give us that is similar to this frequency of love, but it always falls short.

When we hold onto things, feelings, or memories, we shut off the valve to our Divine Essence and live from a place of scarcity, lack, and fear, instead of abundance, prosperity, and trust. To surrender is to trust that we have encoded within us exactly what we are here on this earth to do. We have encoded upon our soul exactly how we are going to get from point A to point B. It is time to trust that innate wisdom within us; we do have all of the necessary answers and guidance.

This is what surrender calls for: the true release of our minds trying to figure it all out. Remember, our minds do not have all of the information all of the time. When we are being led to surrender, it is from our soul. This appears to be scary to the mind because it has no clue of how things are going to play out, so it designs a way to try to keep us where we are, in our comfort zones.

No more comfort zones. Surrender into what you have already co-created. Trust the process. Try something in a new way, today. If you feel led to surrender, just do it. Only when we experience the euphoria of surrender will it become sustainable. We will be asked to surrender many things, many times, in our lives. When we step out and do it, it just gets easier and easier.

The Lotus Flower
Deep down in the pond sat a little seed. This seed was content being a seed. One afternoon, when the seed was contemplating its

existence, it felt a rumbling in its tummy. This rumbling had happened before, but never had it gone on for so long and so powerfully. Suddenly, the seed burst out and began growing downward even deeper into the earth, as well as upward, through the water, toward the light in the sky.

One day, the stem of the new plant emerged from within the water and, with one huge breath, it blossomed into a lotus flower, resting on top of the water. The leaves opened up to absorb the radiant sunshine, as the pure white lotus flower emerged from her womb. The seedling set forth on a remarkable journey from the bottom of the muddy pond to the open sky on top of the water.

Open and radiating, the lotus flower is perfect. There is a wonderful aspect of the flower that unites its existence with a message for all to receive. The entire plant lives in water, as the leaves and flower reside on the surface of the water. Although this is the case, the leaves of the flower do not hold water upon them. The lotus flower reminds us to be grounded in this world, but free, and to exist not of it.

Be a seed. Nurture your seed with love, water, sunshine. Allow your seed to grow at its own pace. Be still, when it is time to be still. Grow, when it is time to grow. Keep focused on the journey. Remain awake during the journey. Feed your seedling with kindred love. Dig your roots deep into the earth. Grow toward the light. Blossom into your fullest potential. Rest. Eat well. Love yourself. Emerge from the depths into the illuminated sky. Be still. Just be. Let go. Stay awake. Close your petals to conserve energy. Open your petals to invite in pure energy. Give a petal to those that need it. Be open to movement and change. Ask for what you need, and trust that you will receive it. Love yourself. Allow yourself to transition into whatever form is in your Highest Good. Know that you have your own unique scent. You are only responsible for your own growth. Grow. Smile. Share from your heart. Speak from your heart. Know that you are interconnected with All That Is. Blow in the wind, you are free. Release when it is time. Come back, and do it all over again. Go buy some seeds, and plant them today.

Today, surrender all the old ways that no longer serve your Highest Good. Surrender all of your old habits that do not lift you up to your best life. Surrender to Living Your Best Life today.

Self-Love
- Remain in the Now.
- I am residing in this moment with love, joy, and peace.
- Cultivate Union with Universal Energy.
- Realize you are ALWAYS connected, it is just time to remember.
- Go with Universal Flow.
- You were born as this Flow; Surrender to its Beauty and Perfection.

I am going to take this moment to acknowledge you for ALL that you have been through this lifetime. At this point in your life, I am certain that you are doing an amazing job at going inward. Every day that you wake up and choose to live with more awareness than the day before, you should smile. You are making great strides every day, and I am very proud of you.

I am acknowledging you right now for all the people in your life who have never seen you for what you have contributed, times you have stuck your neck out for another, love you give that gets unnoticed, hours you put in to raise the children of the world, and times you wanted to give up, but persevered. Together, let's let go of all the hurt and pain that others inflicted upon you because they did not know how to be there for you. This moment is a wonderful opportunity for us, collectively, to set free the angry, hate-filled, negative energies, wrapped around our individual hearts and the heart of this earth.

The seed of Truth, of Who You Really Are, is within you. If you continue to search outside of yourself, you will never find it. You must be willing to go to the stillness that knows no movement: your soul. When we are out of touch with the feeling of love, then how can we be in touch with our Authentic Self? First, we must get back in touch with what love feels like.

I invite you today to take these questions with you, and answer them throughout the week:
- *What did love look like to you as a child?*
- *How were you shown, and how did you express, love as a child?*
- *How did you receive love as an adolescent?*
- *When did you experience your first love?*
- *What does love look and feel like to you, as an adult?*
- *Who do you have in your life that gives you love?*
- *Do you know how to feel Divine Love?*
- *What is your intention today around love?*
- *When you are supported, how does it feel?*
- *What are new ways you can ask for and receive love into your life?*
- *Do you feel that you are open or closed down in your heart chakra?*
- *Are you willing to open up your heart again to unconditional love?*

Do you:
- *Have a strong intention to love and be loved?*
- *Know the difference between wanting something and being ready to receive it?*

- *Consider the notion that you are connected to everyone and everything?*
- *Intellectualize your feelings?*
- *Want the best that love has to offer?*

Have you:
- *Been willing to surrender FULLY to the risk of love?*
- *Allowed yourself to be fully immersed in knowing and being known by another human?*
- *Learned to be vulnerable and undefended while, at the same time, 100 percent authentic and true to yourself?*
- *Consciously expanded your capacity to love and be loved as a goal that you can call your own?*

Are you:
- *Willing to grow yourself beyond the person you are today?*
- *Open to drawing in others who are able to bring the best of who they are to you?*
- *Open FULLY to give and receive love?*
- *Cultivating a sense of belonging, and being honest with yourself that you have a need for others?*
- *Living a conscious, Divine, purpose-driven life?*

Where are you:
- *Calling in nurturing and support into your life?*
- *Feeling connected, valued, cared for, and respected?*
- *In trusting that the possibilities of love in your life are limitless?*
- *In believing that if you just open yourself up and start trusting yourself and others, more goodness and love will flow into your life?*

Love is the foundation of this earth. If we do not feel love, we are not really living.

Love is our natural essence; it is time to call it in.

Next, write out a list of everything that you LOVE. Feel what it is like when you have these experiences of LOVE in your life. Get into the feeling place of love. When you do this, you are aligning your soul with your intention of receiving love. Joy, bliss, love, and serenity are all good examples of a higher vibration. Any time you are living from anything less than these qualities, ask yourself which is a richer experience?

With your list, ask your soul to support you on your journey inward to love. Send one person a day pure love from your heart chakra to theirs. Extend this out to the entire globe, as you ask for all to serve the Highest Good of All That Is.

If we put love into everything that we do and say, we begin to see how Heaven can be lived here on earth. If we are going to evolve into a new paradigm, we must do things out of love, which is the foundation of All That Is. May you see the benefits of living from a place of pure love. If you feel you are far from living from love, realize that the ultimate love is right inside of you. Just ask for it to be shown to you, and it will be.

It is time to return to loving yourself fully. The ultimate goal of life is to realize your True Self. There are many ways and roads to realizing this self, yet there is only one way that will get you there the quickest: the road of LOVE. I invite you to love yourself 100 percent more each day than the previous.

The Presence of Peace is within Us All
- Call in Support from Everywhere in Your Life.
- ALWAYS Come from a Place of SELF-LOVE.
- Be the God/Goddess that you were born to be. Live your fullest potential.
- Always Be in a State of Self-Reflection.
- State Your Intentions and Let Go.

- Leave the "HOW TO's" to the Universe. Be still and trust Divine Timing.
- Be Open to ALL of life's Infinite Possibilities.
- It will change your life.

Peace is within us all, it is our natural essence. Where else will you find peace if not within? Just be quiet, do not engage in any thoughts, and you will feel how free you are. Who AM I? Inquire within. Be still. All will be revealed, but you must first be quiet.

I heard this story about peace, and I wanted to share it with you.

There were two men passing through a town where they decided to bunk for a few nights. The first man was easily irritated the first evening by all of the dogs that were barking incessantly. That night, he went into the second man's room and said, "Are you not disturbed by the noise of the dogs barking?" The second man replied, "I do not hear it as noise but rather as a symphony of music to my ears." The first man got even more irritated because he was looking for a solution. The second night came around and the same thing happened. By the third night, the first man had not slept much at all and was extremely agitated. He entered the room of the second man and before he could utter a word, the second man spoke, "Dear friend, the dogs are chanting a rhythm that can only be felt from the still space of your heart. Sit here with me, and feel the passion of their music. Sit here in silence, and listen. Do not be stirred, and if you are, go into that which caused the stir. Does it not come from the same place?" Since the first man was at his breaking point, he decided to go into his agitation. As he did, he felt an amazing sense of relief. What he had been avoiding all along by engaging in the anger was actually what he was yearning for, peace. By allowing himself to face and go into the emotion of agitation, he allowed his True Essence to arise. He began to hear the orchestrated sounds of music the dogs were making and before he knew it, he was fast asleep.

Today, go into any emotion that arises, and be with it. Go deeper into it. Do not engage it or judge it, just allow it to rise up and dissolve away. Whatever your perspective is, this will be your outcome. Change your perception of one thing today. See it from another's point of view. As the emotion comes up, label it, and set it free. Do not judge, criticize, distort, or edit it, but just allow it to be seen. Just allow it to be.

Living with Integrity

- Realize Clarity as your Birthright.
- Ask and You Shall Receive.
- Return to Source.
- Release the ego and embrace the Creative Realm of Infinity.
- Remain Conscious and Aware.
- Always choose to see life from a state of awareness.
- Be in Harmony with the Invisible Spiritual Energy.
- All thoughts calibrate at a HIGH, FAST frequency, nullifying slower ones.

Integrity is defined as "the state of being entirely whole." Integrity is not as concerned with absolute truths (wrong vs. right), as it is with relative truths (if I say I am love, then it must be in alignment with my actions). A lack of integrity simply suggests that one is being inconsistent and, therefore, disempowered. When there is incongruence within oneself, symptoms begin to arise to point towards these incongruencies going on within. One final leap required for you to move as far away as possible from the old paradigm is to stand in your integrity.

Being in integrity means that first and foremost, you are honest with yourself. When you can be honest with yourself, you can show the world a person who stands powerfully in her integrity and Divine Essence. We all have a past. But, it is only a wounded past when we decide to hold our pain and stories inside. Find a safe space to let your past out so you can set it free. Create a new version of yourself that is clear, pure, and in alignment with your Highest Good.

Ask yourself these questions and be honest about your answers:

What is going on right now that I am being dishonest about?
Example: I tell everyone everything is ok when really it is not.

How does it make me feel when I am not 100 percent honest with my feelings?
Example: I feel sick to my stomach.

What secret(s) am I harboring that I am ready to reveal and set free?
Example: I had an affair.

What stories do I tell others to avoid my true feelings?
Example: I tell them I have it all figured out.

In what areas of my life am I NOT standing in integrity?
Example: At work, with my husband, myself.

What qualities do I need to possess to stand in my integrity and be empowered?
Example: I need the courage and strength to speak my truth.

When you do not express your feelings authentically, they get repressed.

Today, I invite you to do a mask ritual. You will need three blank sheets of paper and a pen, colored pencils, or markers.

1. On the first sheet, I want you to draw a mask. Label this mask: "How I Present Myself to the World." Be honest, as this mask is only for you. Create it to be how you show yourself to the outside world.

2. On the second sheet of paper, I want you to title it: "How I Really Feel about Myself." On this mask, I want you to show how you really feel inside. Place your payoffs on this mask, as well as all of your limiting beliefs. This mask is you being honest and in your integrity. Everyone has secrets they are keeping because they think that it would cause disharmony in one way or another if they told the truth.

3. For today, I invite you to write out your deepest secrets on this mask.

    Now, I want you to look at both of your masks and be honest with how they are making you feel. What is coming up for you? Are the two in close alignment with one another or are they two different people? Look at what you feel you express to the world versus how you really feel.

4. Now, I want you to take a third piece of paper and create a mask labeled: "Who I Really Choose to Be." On this mask, create who you dream or believe you want to be. Here, you will add all of your personal value and how you want to be seen in the world. When you are finished, I would like for you to take your first and second masks and burn them. It is your intention to transmute away all the lies, misconceptions, fears, doubts, stresses, and anything that represents the old paradigm of thinking and being. I want you to be very focused and intentional while you burn

away the old façade of who you used to identify yourself as being.

5. I want you to color in the new mask that represents Who You Really Are. Place this mask where you can see it every day until you are living from this essence 100 percent.

Using Discernment Instead of Judgment

- Sacrifice What You Are for What You Are to Become.
- Stay in Loving Kindness with Your Always-Expanding Source.
- Know that all things are being created by your Divine Creator Self.
- Realize You are NEVER Alone.
- You have legions of angels, spirit guides, and Divine help awaiting you to ask them to come forth into your life and show you your authentic LIFE.
- Intend to Attract Divine Relationships into Your Life.
- Let go of unproductive relationships and be open to empowering ones.
- Rest in the Radiance of Your Open Heart.

Making a judgment is forming an opinion after consideration or deliberation, or using your mental ability to perceive and distinguish relationships. Using discernment means to exhibit keen insight. If we are living in the old paradigm, we are always using our mental thoughts to judge the world around us. When we live in the new paradigm, we use discernment to distinguish between what serves our Highest Good and what does not. When we judge, we close off the channels of acceptance.

Discernment, on the other hand, is using our inner gut feeling to distinguish if a relationship, job, etc. is in our best interest. Using discernment means we are listening inward and following our inner guidance. Judging is a viewpoint from the mind that is always limiting.

Let's pretend that a friend humiliated you in front of many of your friends. You were so hurt that you stopped communicating with her altogether. A year passes, and she calls you up to hang out with you again. Now, one of two things happens: You still feel bitter and want nothing to do with her, or you feel ready to let her back into your life. Let's say that your gut feeling says you do not want her to come back into your life. You start to question why you feel this way when you are "supposed" to be a loving and forgiving person.

This is where discernment comes in. When you discern a situation, you are using your intuition. You are also being asked to marry your intuitive guidance with speaking your Truth. What happens when you are being asked to discern is that your guidance is showing you how to play your role as actor or actress consciously in the other person's life.

For so long, you have been using your mental mind to figure things out. Inside, you do not feel right about the situation, but you turn to your rational mind and convince yourself that it is ok to hang out with that person. After a month, you find out that she has been talking badly about you behind your back. Your intuition told you that this person was up to no good, but your rational mind said it was ok. Your mind told you that you were judging the situation and to stop judging and hang out with her. However, your intuition was asking you to discern the situation, using keen insight to decide if it served your Highest Good to hang out with your old friend.

Inquire within about discerning situations versus judging them. When we utilize our intuitive muscle and follow its guidance, we come from a win/win perspective, honoring each other's Highest Good. People do have hidden agendas, and using your intuitive discerning energy guides you away from those who might otherwise wish to play games and cause you harm. Using your discernment is holding a higher vibration of integrity and Divine Love. Practice using your discernment over judgment and you will begin to see the results immediately.

Creating a Win/Win World

- Move Through Life as if Your Body is in Perfect Health.
- I am healed. I am healthy. I am whole.
- Realize You Have All the Time You Need.
- Be Open to Seeing Your Life from a New Perspective.
- Change the way you look at things and the things you look at will change.
- Cultivate Compassion.
- I am love. I am loved. I am love.
- Give of Yourself. Always Be in Service to the Greater Whole.

All experiences are neutral. When you have a set belief about something, then you have already set the course for a reaction or a response. When your belief is set in a space of love and win/win, your view of the event becomes neutral. When your belief is set in the fixed automatic mode, you react from a subconscious level. This reaction usually comes from a place of fear and doubt. When we recall that all events are neutral, we become the observer to the event. We take responsibility for our own actions and decide how we wish to respond to the event.

You may not realize how much of this world revolves around a win/lose philosophy. When we are born with amnesia of Who We Really Are and our mind is constructed to always be in survival mode, it seems natural to create win/lose situations.

The dynamics of this world reflect win/lose in so many different arenas. If you have not figured it out by now, living from your Authentic Self means that you will have to live a different song than the song of humanity. You will need to live the song of your Divinity, the part of you that knows only how to create a world that is win/win. This is one of the greatest lessons for you to learn and integrate.

If you decide to transcend the win/lose game, then you rise above it to the state of being humble. When you are humble, you view life from a Higher Self perspective of win/win. Life happens, but you do not judge it or make yourself or another wrong or bad because of it. If a situation highlights your ego, then you can see it as an observer and choose to become your True Self in that moment by being humbled. It is time to stop the win/lose game.

The Highest Vision is that you set your intention every morning.

Recite the following:

My intention is to live my life from a win/win attitude. I am stilling my mind so I can feel and hear my guidance. It is my intention to live from my Highest Design where all exists as a creation where we are all related and connected. Therefore, I am asking for a win/win in this specific situation occurring in my life, as well as always. Remind me gracefully when I am coming from a win/lose perspective. Gently show me what a win/win outcome will look and feel like. When I am caught up in my win/lose attitude, please keep showing me a win/win, no matter how stubborn I appear. Blessed Be.

Here is an example of a win/lose and win/win situation:
You get fired from a job:

Win/lose: You blame the people you worked with and do not see how you had anything to do with your being fired. You become angry and begin to conspire against certain people or the whole company.

Win/win: You realize that everything happens for a reason. You ask your guidance what lessons you can learn from the experience. Instead of blaming, you take responsibility and ask to be shown a win/win outcome. You then stay in a current of a higher vibration, learn your lesson easily, and a new, better job shows up immediately.

When you live from a win/lose perspective, you hold a low vibration. When you live from a win/win perspective, you hold a high frequency. If your natural essence is a high frequency, you see how consciously choosing to remain at a high frequency makes it easier for you to listen inward to your high-frequency guidance. If you are continually resonating at a win/lose low-frequency, it is nearly impossible to hear your high-frequency guidance.

Living as Divine Love
- Serve as a Warrior of an Open Heart and Liberated Spirit.
- Find your Voice and Speak your Truth.
- Realize the Universal Source Supplies Everything.
- You get everything you need (personally, financially, spiritually, emotionally, mentally) exactly when you need it.
- Live in Alignment with Abundance and Prosperity.
- Breathe in the abundance of Oxygen every moment and know this as Abundance and Prosperity.

Please remember that our natural essence is Divine Love, a love that is untouched by any of our life's experiences. Only you can inquire within and reach this feeling. It is at the depths of your being where it has remained, quietly, as you have danced all around it, searching.

Below you will find a list of attitudes and qualities that we are all capable of engendering. Be open to the possibilities that lie ahead for you and to embodying each one of these possibilities fully, if you are not already:

- You no longer care what others think about you because your focus is inward.
- You become an observer of your life. With this focus, you realize that everyone is an actor or an actress playing out a part so that you may know your True Self.
- You begin to accept people for who they are playing their part to be. You know that they are doing a great job at their role.
- You begin to clear out all that no longer serves your Highest Good and naturally draw into your life all that serves your Highest Good.
- You get out of your own way and let the Will of Heaven flow through you.
- You easily stay focused on your own path because you know that by listening within you will always know when and where to go and what to do, in any given moment.
- You realize that this journey starts with you taking care of what your innate wisdom guides you to do. You no longer deplete your energy by putting others' needs before your own. You understand what this means, knowing it is not a selfish act, but an empowering one.
- There is no more drama because you handle all that comes your way with grace and ease.
- You are no longer attached to the outcome because you trust that all is in Divine Order.
- You crave simplicity in all things and require, and thrive on, simple processes, simple desires, and a very simple lifestyle.

- You are empowered to manifest your visions and dreams in physical ways.
- You perceive the world of different possibilities and believe all things are possible.
- You declare yourself and show your true colors, having the courage to be yourself.
- You take great flights of the mind and then integrate your wisdom into your daily life.
- You feel and see your place in this world and begin to see life as even more synchronistic and amazing every day.
- Stillness is the only way for you. You are a beacon of light holding space for all those that are walking their paths perfectly.
- You know God's Will and your will are One.
- There is a balance between your channel of receiving and your channel of giving. Both are open and clear.
- You are sending love to the universe and everything in it, daily.
- You know that all of your needs are met and always will be. You know that everyone gets exactly what they need exactly when they need it.
- You realize your true teacher is your inner teacher and you trust your guidance fully.
- You begin to feel a unity with Source greater than ever before. This is reflected in your community of friends and new ways of relating to your family.
- Your surrounding environment has no effect on you because you no longer take things personally. Nothing is worth getting that upset about anymore because you see the value everything brings into your life.
- You have surrendered your idea of what being in control looks like. You trust that all is in Divine order.

- You have a heightened compassion for all living things. You continue to experience higher states of Divine love and joy.
- You begin to lead by example, from a place of power and from within power, instead of power over.
- You only desire to do what is innately yours to do. You no longer have a large mundane "to do" list of responsibilities.
- You begin to have an understanding about how everything is connected. You understand that there are no mistakes, all is in Divine right order, and there was never anything "wrong."
- You speak with an inner conviction that the Universal Source supplies everything.
- You are always in a state of gratitude, bewilderment, and appreciation.
- You live in the present moment, aware of your inner peace.
- You believe in your unique genius, and you are inspired to produce from it what is in your fullest potential to produce.

It is time to release the old vision of what we USED to be or how we USED to see our self. We do not have to be this person anymore if we choose to set her/him free. This is the moment to reclaim our innocent guiding light. It has spoken and it is waiting for us to come home—-where the soul resides, where the heart is. Home, where we begin to receive clarity from our inner voice that knows what is in our best interest. Home, where we listen to our guidance and put its teachings into action, trusting the Divine Essence of Who We Really Are. I invite you to take a risk and make the choice to live fully from the new paradigm. Choose one of the above qualities and fully embody it. After you have embodied one, choose another, and keep going until you are fully immersed in the new paradigm existing fully from Divine Love.

Chapter Eight

My Personal Message to You Remembering Your Essence

The journey of the heart must be taken inward. The person who looks outside is just dreaming. If you go within, then you will feel the wonder of what this book is all about. Wisdom is gained by living from the fruit of your essence. What you have longed to become is what you have always been. The one who looks inside, awakens. You have come a long way on your journey through the darkness to reach the light. What has always remained true and constant within your heart is the magnificence of Who You Really Are.

The only way to feel this essence 100 percent is to finally drop all of your thoughts and return home: Home, where the heart is. You have legions of Divine Love and Light surrounding you. You are this Divine Love. You incarnated to live out your destiny, to own your full magnificence while on earth. It is time for you to consciously rekindle a state of Divine Love.

Your soul has encoded upon it exactly what you are here on earth to do. When you let go of your fears and worries about how you are going to get this, do that, or be, you will find what you have always been searching for. When you can let go for even an instant, your Divine Essence will be right there, untouched by any of your life's experiences.

By allowing your mind to dive back into your heart, you go from doing to being. In the space of being, you never need to know what to do. It is only the mind that tells you that you need to know. Yet, when you are in the space between doing and being, you are given an opportunity to open. Whenever you find that you are in a place where you don't know what to do, just surrender and OPEN UP.

Which is crazier: Diving into Divine Love or denying Divine Love? This choice presents itself to us each and every day. It is time to just stop the story, drop it for good, and open to what our innate wisdom has to offer us.

Everything in this book has a purpose for being written down. Each piece can take you through the baby steps of awakening or you can just leap fully into the wonder of All That Is. Either road will take you Home. Both are perfect.

It is my heartfelt prayer that you fully recognize the permanent source of fulfillment already present in the core of your being. Become centered in your core. Ask your inner self, your soul, to guide you. Express your desire to feel your Divine Self; it is your truest essence. Go inside to that space where your heart resides, where your life force sits in silence. Open up to your inner being as you allow the feeling of pure love to envelope you. Focus on your heart chakra, as you are bathed in pure Divine Love.

Who You Really Are is completely whole and totally free. You are already that which you longed for most. To realize your True Self is to totally Be. You are right where you need to be as all is in perfect Divine Order. It is time to step inward to where the Truth of Who You Really Are resides. This journey into the unknown cannot be figured out. Just trust that this book has been brought into your life for a reason. Allow the reason to unfold in perfect magnificence. You are very loved in every moment. Awaken today to this Divine Love that is within you. Pay it forward by shining your Brilliant Light into the world. One person does make a difference and that one person is you.

My Story

When I was six weeks old, I was diagnosed with spinal meningitis. In the early 70's, doctors were not certain which strain of antibiotics would cure this particular type of meningitis. As my small body lay lifeless in an incubator for days, my mother and father would come and place their hands inside the tube and hold my hand as they prayed for their little angel to recover. The prognosis was not good for me, and the doctors told my family that I would most likely be a vegetable or blind or deaf for the rest of my life.

One morning, my parents arrived at the hospital as a nurse approached them: "Mr. and Mrs. Canull, we wanted to let you know that your daughter stopped breathing twice last night in her sleep. We thought she was gone and then, all of a sudden, she started breathing again." The doctors were not sure I was going to make it through another night, so my family arranged to have me baptized in the hospital's church that day.

While I was being prepared to be baptized, my spirit traveled back through the portal up to a bright light. I played with my angel friends and told them that I missed them. They reminded me that I had a very important mission on earth and that I needed to go back and be in my body. I was sad because they were my very best friends, and I saw that when I would be on earth, people would not understand me for who I was. My angel friends reassured me that when I returned to earth school, they would always be right beside me. They sent me forth on a golden ray of light back down to earth.

Right before I re-entered my body, I heard them whisper, "Kelly, you will remain awake and conscious of Who You Really Are; this is your destiny. We love you, and soon you will be able to hear us again. Your purpose is to remind others of the innate wisdom stored within their souls." Bam! I was back in my body and had made a full recovery. My family and the doctors were amazed that I had pulled through just when they thought that this night was going to be my last on earth. From that point on, there was something different about me that my family noticed, too.

As a child, I would sit and meditate on the couch to get all the thoughts out of my head. At the age of seven, I was writing twenty-page stream of consciousness papers. The teacher at school would call my mother and me in for a private conference because the stories never made any logical sense! My mother was aware enough to see that I was producing stream of consciousness writings that flowed from my heart and soul. I saw it as my way of communicating with my angel friends. I remember sitting up at night and asking them to come down and play with me. I knew they were always there, so I would write to them. All of my papers in those years were about God, love, angels, and Heaven on earth.

As a child, I related better to adults than children. I was able to sense things before they happened. I was able to relate to animals in a deep, telepathic way. I used to take horseback riding lessons, and I would love to go early so I could talk with the horses. I knew when people were not being honest with me. I was able to get to the core of things without people having to say much to me. I was different than any of my friends or the adults I came across. I always felt a strong inner drive to stay true to my Authentic Self and not get drawn into the drama and illusions of the outer world. My best friends were the angels and the elementals in nature.

When I was eleven, a cousin of mine passed away in a motorcycle accident. When I heard the news, I had this instant feeling inside that I wanted to talk with him. One day, my mother and aunt called me into the room where they were trying out something called "automatic writing." In that moment, I felt a sensation that flowed through my entire body. I was finally going to get the chance to communicate with my deceased cousin! My mother explained that they had read about automatic writing, but that they were not having any success getting the pen to move. I took the pen in my hand and it began writing without my moving it. I was so happy that now I had a way to communicate with my cousin and my angel friends.

From the ages of twelve to fifteen, I used the pen and paper as a way to communicate with deceased loved ones to provide personal readings for family and friends. I used the tool of automatic writing to bring clarity, wisdom, and insight to those who surrounded me, providing comfort and peace through the messages conveyed through me.

When I was fifteen, I was at a friend's house where her mother had invited a "psychic" in from California. My friend and I gathered with her mother and the psychic to levitate a table. I had no idea what we were supposed to be doing and was not sure if it would work. All of a sudden, the woman said, "I have never experienced this before, but I am not receiving any guidance." Suddenly I heard a voice within my head that started sharing insights with me to tell the mother and daughter. I quickly said, "Well, I am hearing something." I kept hearing a voice talk with a soft tone that began sharing more information with me to convey to the others. Before that moment, I had always used the pen and paper to bring forth information. Now, I was hearing, seeing, sensing, and being given an all around knowingness about the message. It was just as my angels promised—that someday I would hear them again.

At the age of twenty-one, I graduated from college and decided I was going to be a psychic or Messenger for the Soul. I continued bringing messages from the other side to hundreds of people. Eventually, I began bringing people clarity and guidance for their own lives. I began connecting in with the souls or the Higher Self of others, bringing messages from their souls.

I took a personal vow to only work with pure Love and Light. I made sure that when I was delivering messages to others that it was from the Highest Source and always in alignment with their Highest Good. I began communicating with a deeper sense of peace and love. My new passion became bringing Divine Love to others through connecting in with their Higher Self and the angelic realm to bring forth guidance to all that entered my life.

Eventually, I realized that certain clients were coming back on a regular basis. Normally that would be good for business, but for me it meant that people were becoming dependent upon me and the guidance I shared. I saw it as a problem that people were depending on me instead of listening to their own inner guidance. I also noticed a common theme that everyone brought forth, no matter what their life circumstances: They were choosing fear over love.

So, in 2001, I decided to start coaching people on how to realign their body, mind, and soul so they could receive guidance on their own. I designed a program that coaches people through the process of getting back in touch with their internal guidance systems: the Voice of their Souls. This process proved successful as people learned how to pose their own questions to their soul, or Higher Self, and receive clarity and guidance that day in relation to their inquiry. I noticed that people were becoming more empowered as they stopped looking outside of themselves for answers and starting inquiring within.

I noticed that when a person begins to apply their own innate wisdom into their life, they naturally shift out of fear and into Divine Love. The results that I have seen have inspired me to continue guiding people to go inward through my personal Soul Readings as well as the wisdom I have shared in this book.

Sometimes our journey requires us to take baby steps, while other times it gives us opportunities to take leaps and bounds. This book is an integration of both of these ways. On my own personal journey of awakening, I have taken both baby steps and leaps and bounds. This book is about the awareness that I have gained and lived by walking forward in each and every moment with my soul as the leader. I did this despite the beliefs of those outside of myself. I did it because I have always felt a deep inward pull reminding me that there was always more to be unveiled. Do you have the same feeling pulling at your heart strings reminding you that there is something more than what you are currently viewing as your reality?

I share the following with you as an example of what awakening to Who I Really Am looked like to me. I invite you to see the reflection of your own life's journey in this process as well.

1. First, I was born and had full amnesia of Who I Really Am. I lived a semi-normal life where family, friends, culture, and my society influenced me. I believed what others outside of myself said that I was, and I developed my personality self out of this model that I was shown.

2. Around the age of 10, I began to feel an inward stirring that was telling me that there was certainly

something more than what my church, family, and community outside of myself was teaching me. This is where I began my first conscious phase of awakening. I offered my innermost thoughts to the world through poetry and stream of consciousness stories. I felt there was something greater to be pursued; I just did not know what it looked like. I simply followed what felt right.

3. The stirring for more continued to rear its head as the years went on. Eventually, I decided that I was ready to drop what was unfulfilling in my life to search for what would be fulfilling. This phase was where I started to read self-help books, go to workshops, attend psychic fairs, and look to others for guidance. I surrounded myself with people who could guide me in ways that my current model of the world could not. This stage is when I became aware, through clairaudience, of the unseen realm all around me.

4. My next phase was to take all of the knowledge I had gained from these classes and put the practices into action. This stage was experiential instead of just knowledge-driven. Here is where I first became aware of myself-defeating thoughts. I consciously watched every word out of my mouth, and when I did not like what I said, I would change it. Consciously shifting my thoughts from disempowering to empowering was extremely helpful to me.

5. The next phase was where I decided to take 100 percent responsibility for my past. I started to see that everyone on this planet is an actor or an actress playing out a part so that I could know myself better. I

started to see that my past was just a story and that all I needed to do was to drop the story and not pick it back up again. I remained at this phase for a very long time because I did not fully grasp what "letting go" really entailed. This was my baby-step phase of awakening. I kept picking my story back up because I did not know what to do once I dropped it. After years of doing this, I was exhausted and finally dropped all of my stories for good.

6. One day, I was so fed up that I just decided to fully surrender. When I did this, I began to not take things personally, as I learned to just observe my thoughts as "just thoughts" and not integral to Who I Really Am. By doing this, I stopped giving my thoughts the power to control my life and began inviting them inward to my soul. My mind became humbled. In this humbleness, it surrendered and sunk back into my soul, where it became the servant to my heart, instead of ruling it.

7. As my mind became still, I began to feel something inside of me that had never left me since my birth: Divine Love. It was this feeling of pure Divine Love that I focused all of my attention on. As I did this, my emotions and thoughts would still rise and fall, but I would not identify myself by or with them. I just allowed them to pass by, knowing they were just like clouds passing in the sky.

8. One day I reached a point where I had to meet death fully. This was a time in my life where I knew that this meeting with death meant that I had to go into the unknown 100 percent. This step was both terrifying

and liberating. I stood at that door of death for a very long time until I was fed up enough with not feeling totally fulfilled from within. Then, I just stepped into death and let it bathe me with its emptiness. There was nothing there: no thought, no emotions, no past, and no future. Death was the void of the unknown that my whole being had been waiting for since it had last remembered it in the womb.

9. As I went into death 100 percent, I came through onto the other side. I found that for me, personally, true fullness resides on the other side of death: This place is where the mind only knows stillness and everything is effortless. The new paradigm lives here. I had come home to the full resonance with the Truth of Who I Really Am.

I share this personal process with you because it is a universal process. The times are changing, and we do not have to be in the dark any longer as to what is ahead on this road of awakening. This book is designed to show you how to get back in touch with your soul, the place where all of your innate wisdom resides.

Now, take a look at your own life and what phase of awakening you are in. My story is the same as your story. We were born as innocent Light. The dust of our stories covered this Light, and now we must uncover it. Through this process, that which has always been within us is revealed.

The following is list of things that have helped me stay true to my soul. Do not look at them as me telling you what to do, but rather in the form of your soul speaking to you:
- Be totally honest with yourself.
- Be willing to see your life from new perspectives and live from these new places.

- Be open to loving something more than just your personal life.
- Be willing to go deeply inward, beyond where you are today.
- Give up living in the future, and reside in this moment.
- Be willing to experiment with new ideas and just see what happens.
- Stop the searching, and be fully raw in the unknown.
- Realize that 99 percent of your commentary is a lie, so be willing to stop the commentary on all of your stories—immediately.

Now, I would like to share with you more ways I have learned to keep my soul alive. I have written these affirmations from a first person or "I" point of view. This way you can read them out loud to yourself, claiming them as your own:

- Each day, I call in only what I DO WANT, as my essence, into my life.
- I ask my angels and spirit guides a daily question and know that I will receive clarity in return.
- I allow only positive statements to be honored when they are in my thoughts. I state out loud at least three positive statements each day, so I may keep my mind focused on empowering thoughts.
- I imagine a pillar of gold light flowing through all of my cells. I tell my body that I am grateful for it and all my cells for working in perfect order, every day.
- I send the world Divine Love, and say thanks for everything that happened in my day. I ask for clarity on any subject that I may be questioning. I ask that I am shown guidance in my dreams, or throughout my day.

- I send gratitude to each of my body parts.
- I send love and light from my heart chakra into the heart of the earth, and then I watch it stream from the ocean to the tiniest stream. I then imagine that this is the same love and light that is streaming through all of my veins.
- I recite the following: "Divine Angels, Masters, Ascended Masters, and Spirit Guides, please surround me in white light. Please surround me with a white light of protection so only the Highest Divine Essence will flow through me. I send pure love and light into the world today. Blessed Be."
- I place different pictures all around my house that remind me of peace and tranquility.
- I tell someone every day how much I love and appreciate who they are.
- When self-doubt creeps in, I go lie down on my bed and call in Divine Love to fill my heart. I do not engage in any thought. I imagine this golden love filling every core of my being. I give myself permission to feel, instead of think.
- I trust my intuition 100 percent, every day.
- I make time every day to be outside in nature. When it is just too darn cold for me, I allow myself to go within to my own inner nature.
- I follow my guidance always and trust that I will always be taken care of. I honor my inner guidance and allow the universe to provide me with what I need, both in the lessons and the tangible manifestations.
- I keep a clean living environment to reflect my inner sanctuary of peace.
- I live simply, recycling and re-using.

- I live with integrity. I face my truth with an authenticity that reassures me that no matter what I have to say, all will be fine.
- I am unattached to the outcome. I put my heart's desires out to the universe, and then I let go. I am unattached to how or when these desires show up. I trust that the Higher Self of Who I Really Am knows what is in my best interest.
- I realize that living my Authentic Self takes a full-time commitment to living. I lead by example and love that feeling.
- I live more fully in the present by dropping my "to do" list. I trust that by being present, my intuition will tell me, guide me, or show me whatever it is that I need to attend to in any given moment.
- I pay attention to the body/mind/spirit connection. When my body is out of balance, I can tell. I then inquire within as to what it is trying to tell me. I listen when I need to sleep and do not resist taking a midday nap when I really need it.
- I ask for, and am open to receive, support from others.
- I allow the natural cycles of life to be. When I am in a major learning curve, I realize that I need to give myself extra "me time" to integrate the new wisdom I am receiving. When I give myself space, this wisdom assimilates much easier because I am giving it an open valve by which to enter my life.
- I no longer judge myself, nor do I believe any negative thoughts my ego may slip in once in awhile. I exist with a stillness of the mind.
- I make sure that my words and actions are in alignment.
- I am fully open to change.

- I walk through my process, even when resistance comes up.
- I identify what I do want and dream BIG!
- I ground my emotional, physical, mental, and spiritual bodies in the Here and Now, being 100 percent in my body with awareness.
- I trust and surrender.
- I focus on empowering stories to inspire, motivate, and guide me.
- I cry when I feel like it, and I laugh when I feel like it.

These affirmations reflect ways I have experienced a peaceful state of existence. Take a moment and choose just one. Focus on this one for a week, and see how it plays out more fully in your life. I wrote these affirmations out in the first person so that you can also read them and state them as your own. Repeat each one in the first person, and notice how you feel. Blessed Be.

You are a magical soul here on earth to unveil your gifts to this world. Surrender with me today, and open up to the infinite possibilities that lie ahead for you. I stand beside you as a pillar of light, unconditionally loving you. You are here reading this book right now because you are ready to live from your Divine Essence, once again. I support you on your journey, standing beside you as your equal. I am here to be a constant pillar of love as you continue your journey inward. Take off your armor, set down your façade, and begin to dance to the innate rhythms of your soul. Together, let's empower each other to **Listen** inwardly to our soul, **Live** out our guidance, and **Lead** by example. Let's join our brilliant lights and live our best life.

Thank you for taking this inward journey with me. Namaste.

Upon this night,
Do not hold tight.
Always be
Ever so free.
Knowing within,
Your heart so strong,
That you could never
Ever be wrong.
Know you are ever so bright,
Beaming strongly thy powerful light.
Peace, dear child,
Surrounds you so tight.
Be ever so present,
So pure and so bright.
For in the essence of life so grand
It is thy Light for which you stand.
Everything will end in love because everything was
created in love.

Acknowledgment

I would like to acknowledge everyone who has walked before me, beside me and behind me. I am grateful for all that you have done to help shift this world out of the old paradigm and into the new paradigm.

About the Author

Kelly Canull currently lives in Boulder, Colorado with her greatest teachers: her chocolate lab, Tessa, and golden retriever, Piper. In addition to all the wisdom Kelly provides within this book, she also offers personal Soul Readings where she brings forth guidance and wisdom from the Voice of your Soul.

She uses this gift as a way to jump start you back in tune and in touch with the Voice of your Soul so that you can realize the Truth of Who You Really Are. Kelly's intention is to guide you deeply into your Center—to fan the spark of creative awakening and deepen a connection to the creative Source within. By connecting you to the Voice of your Soul, a channel is created for wisdom to flow. Kelly brings Divine Love into everything she does, reminding us all to do the same.

You can read more about what Kelly has to offer this world through her website: www.KellyCanull.com or you can contact her personally at: AnInwardJourney@gmail.com.

LaVergne, TN USA
07 March 2010
175222LV00003B/14/P